麦格希 中英双语阅读文库

一生必读的名著

第1辑

【美】马克·吐温 (Mark Twain)　【英】笛福 (Daniel Defoe) ●著

李进彪　刘庆双●译

麦格希中英双语阅读文库编委会●编

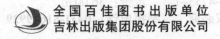

全国百佳图书出版单位
吉林出版集团股份有限公司

图书在版编目（CIP）数据

一生必读的名著. 第1辑 /(美) 马克·吐温
(Mark Twain) , (英) 笛福 (Daniel Defoe) 著；麦格
希中英双语阅读文库编委会编；李进彪, 刘庆双译. --2版. --
长春 : 吉林出版集团股份有限公司, 2018.3（2022.1重印）
（麦格希中英双语阅读文库）
ISBN 978-7-5581-4753-1

Ⅰ.①一… Ⅱ.①马… ②笛… ③麦… ④李… ⑤刘
… Ⅲ.①英语—汉语—对照读物②世界文学—作品综合集
Ⅳ.①H319.4：Ⅰ

中国版本图书馆CIP数据核字(2018)第046825号

一生必读的名著　第1辑

编：麦格希中英双语阅读文库编委会
插　　画：齐　航　李延霞
责任编辑：朱　玲
封面设计：冯冯翼
开　　本：660mm×960mm　1/16
字　　数：226千字
印　　张：10
版　　次：2018年3月第2版
印　　次：2022年1月第2次印刷

出　　版：吉林出版集团股份有限公司
发　　行：吉林出版集团外语教育有限公司
地　　址：长春市福祉大路5788号龙腾国际大厦B座7层
　　　　　邮编：130011
电　　话：总编办：0431-81629929
　　　　　发行部：0431-81629927　0431-81629921(Fax)
印　　刷：北京一鑫印务有限责任公司

ISBN 978-7-5581-4753-1　　　定价：36.00元

前言 *PREFACE*

英国思想家培根说过：阅读使人深刻。阅读的真正目的是获取信息，开拓视野和陶冶情操。从语言学习的角度来说，学习语言若没有大量阅读就如隔靴搔痒，因为阅读中的语言是最丰富、最灵活、最具表现力、最符合生活情景的，同时读物中的情节、故事引人入胜，进而能充分调动读者的阅读兴趣，培养读者的文学修养，至此，语言的学习水到渠成。

"麦格希中英双语阅读文库"在世界范围内选材，涉及科普、社会文化、文学名著、传奇故事、成长励志等多个系列，充分满足英语学习者课外阅读之所需，在阅读中学习英语、提高能力。

◎难度适中

本套图书充分照顾读者的英语学习阶段和水平，从读者的阅读兴趣出发，以难易适中的英语语言为立足点，选材精心、编排合理。

◎精品荟萃

本套图书注重经典阅读与实用阅读并举。既包含国内外脍炙人口、耳熟能详的美文，又包含科普、人文、故事、励志类等多学科的精彩文章。

◎功能实用

本套图书充分体现了双语阅读的功能和优势，充分考虑到读者课外阅读的方便，超出核心词表的词汇均出现在使其意义明显的语境之中，并标注释义。

鉴于编者水平有限，凡不周之处，谬误之处，皆欢迎批评教正。

我们真心地希望本套图书承载的文化知识和英语阅读的策略对提高读者的英语著作欣赏水平和英语运用能力有所裨益。

丛书编委会

Contents

Gulliver's Travels

Part 1 A Journey to Lilliput

Chapter 1 I Come to Lilliput

My father lived in the north of England, but he was not very rich. I was the youngest of five brothers. I left school when I was seventeen years old. My father could not pay for me after that. I travelled on the ship *Antelope* to the South Seas. We left Bristol in May, 1699.

格列佛游记

第一部分 小人国之旅

第一章 来到小人国

我父亲住在英格兰北部，但他并不是很富有。我是五个兄弟中最小的。我十七岁的时候离开了学校。从那以后我的父亲不再供养我。我乘坐"羚羊号"驶向南太平洋。我们于1699年5月离开布里斯托尔。

---

antelope *n.* 羚羊

I will not write down everything about our journey on those seas. But I will tell you this. On our way to the East Indies, a great wind carried us the wrong way. Twelve of our men *died from* the hard work and bad food, and the other men were not very strong.

One morning there was heavy rain and we could not see well. In the strong winds, the ship hit something in the water, and broke. Six of us got a boat into the sea. But we were weak and the wind *turned it over*. We fell into the water.

The wind and the water carried me away from the other men and I never saw them again.

"I'm going to die!" I cried loudly.

But then I put my feet down. I could stand! The wind was weaker

---

我不会写下所有关于我们在海上的旅程。但我要告诉你,我们到东印度群岛时,一场大风使我们走错了路线。我们中的十二人死于艰苦的工作和劣质的食物,而其他人也都不是很强壮。

一天早上,下着大雨,我们看不清楚。在强风中,这艘船撞到海里的什么东西,把船撞破了。我们中的六个人上了一条小船漂流在海上。但是我们很虚弱,风把船吹翻了,我们掉进了水里。

风和水把我带到了远离其他人的地方,后来我再也没有见过他们。

"我要死了!"我大声地喊叫。

但后来我把脚放了下来。我可以站起来!风也变弱了。我在水里走了

---

die from 死于   turn sth over 使翻转

now. I walked for more than a kilometre through the water and came to an island. It was after seven at night. I travelled another half a kilometre, but there were no houses or people. *Perhaps* I could not see them because I was very tired. Then I sat on the ground and slept the best sleep of my life.

I woke up after about nine hours. It was daylight and I was on my back. I tried to stand up, but I could not move! I turned my head a little and looked round me.

I saw thousands of *strings* across my body. They were everywhere — round my arms, my feet and through my long hair! I could only stay there on my back and look up at the sky.

一公里多的路程来到一个岛上。已经晚上七点以后了。我又走了半公里，但这里没有房屋和人。也许因为我太累了所以看不到了他们。于是我坐在地上，睡了我生命中最美好的一觉。

我在大约九小时后醒了过来。已经是白天了，我躺在地上。我试图站起来，但是我不能动！我把头转动了一点向四周打量着。

我看见成千上万的绳子交叉在我身上。到处都是绳子——围绕着我的手臂、脚，并穿过我的长发！我只能躺着，仰望着天空。

---

perhaps *adv.* 也许；可能　　　　　　　　　　　　string *n.* 绳子

The sun was hot, and the light hurt my eyes. I heard *noises* next to me, but I could see nothing. Then something moved on my foot. It moved over my body and up to my face. I looked down and I saw a man. He was smaller than my hand. Forty more little men followed him.

I cried loudly and they were afraid. They all ran away, and jumped onto the ground. Some were hurt, they told me later. They came back, and one man walked near my face. He threw up his hands and looked up at me. He called, "Hekinah degul!" And the other men answered, "Hekinah? Degul hekinah!" I could not understand their language.

I pulled very hard and I got one arm up from the ground. I tried to

---

太阳火辣辣的，阳光刺痛了我的眼睛。我听到身边有响声，但我什么也看不见。然后有东西在我脚上移动。它走过了我的身体来到我的脸上。我往下一看，看到一个人。他比我的手还要小。四十个小人跟在他后面。

我大声喊叫着，他们害怕了。结果他们都跑开了，跳到了地上。他们后来告诉我有一些人受伤了。后来他们又回来了，一个人走近我的脸。他举起双手并抬头看着我。他喊道，"Hekinah degul！"其他人回答说，"Hekinah? Degul hekinah！"我听不懂他们的语言。

我很困难地拉着让一只胳膊从地面起来。我尽自己最大努力想再看

---

noise *n.* 声音；噪音

look at this man again. It hurt, because it pulled some hair out of my head. I put out my hand and tried to catch some little men. But they ran away. Then I heard a noise, and something hurt my hand.

"A thousand small *swords*!" I thought. I looked down. They were *arrows*! Some arrows went into my clothes and I could not feel them. But other arrows went high into the sky and came down on my face. They hurt me and I was afraid for my eyes.

I put my hand over my face. "I'll stay quiet,"I thought. "Then I can break the strings tonight. These people can't hurt me very much — they're too small!"

So I stayed quiet and waited. No more arrows came from the little men, but their noise got louder and louder. "There are more people here now," I thought.

看这个人。因为它扯掉了我的头发所以感觉有些疼。我伸出手想抓几个小人。但他们都逃跑了。然后我听到了什么声音，有东西伤到了我的手。

"是成千支小剑！"我想。我往下一看，是箭！有些箭射进我的衣服里面，但我没什么感觉。但其他箭飞射高空然后落在我的脸上。它们刺痛了我，我很害怕伤到自己的眼睛。

我把手放在脸上。"我要安静地待着，"我想。"然后今晚我可以挣断这些绳子。这些人不能严重伤害到我——他们太小了！"

所以我静静地等待着。小人们没有再放箭，但是他们的声音越来越大。"人越来越多了，"我想。

---

sword *n.* 剑

arrow *n.* 箭

I heard a sound near my ear. I turned my head to the noise and saw men next to me.

"They're building something from wood," I thought. "It's a table!"

Now there were four men on top of it. I understood — they wanted to talk to me.

One of the men on the table was older and larger than the other three. He *wore* a beautiful coat. A little boy, his *servant*, carried the back of this coat above the ground. The older man called, "Langro dehul san." Forty people came and cut the strings round my head. Now I could turn and see the people on the table better.

Then the man in the long coat began to speak. He spoke very well, and he moved his hands up and down. I began to understand

---

　　我听到耳边传来一些声音。我顺着声音的方向转过头，看到有人在我附近。

　　"他们在用木材建造什么，"我想。"是一张桌子！"

　　现在有四个人站在上面。我明白了——他们想跟我说话。

　　桌子上其中一个男人比其他三个年纪要大并且身体更庞大。他穿着一件漂亮的袍子。一个小男孩，他的仆人，托着这件袍子落在地面上的部分。年长者说，"Langro dehul san。"四十个人过来砍断了围绕在我头上的绳子。现在我可以转过来更好地看到桌子上的人了。

　　身穿长袍的人开始说话了。他说得很好，并且双手上下挥舞着。我开始理解他所说的了。他讲了很长一段时间。当然，他的话对我来说很陌

---

wear *v.* 穿 　　　　　　　　　　　　　　　　　　　servant *n.* 仆人

MCGRAW-HILL

him. He spoke for a long time. Of course, his words were strange to me, but I watched his hands.

"We will not hurt you," I understood. "But do not try to run away, or we will *kill* you." I put up my hand and showed him: "I will stay here." Then I had an idea. I put my hand to my mouth: "I am hungry."

The man understood me. He shouted to the people on the ground. A hundred men *climbed* onto my body and walked up to my mouth. They carried food for me. It came from the king, they told me later.

"What food is this?" I thought. "They're giving me very small animals!"

生，但我一直注视着他的手。

"我们不会伤害你的，"我明白了。"但是不要试图逃跑，否则我们会杀了你。"我举起手给他说明："我会留在这里。"然后我有了一个主意。我把手指向嘴："我饿了。"

那人理解了我的意思。他大声对地面上的人喊着。一百多个人爬上我的身体，走近我的嘴。他们拿食物给我吃。他们后来告诉我那是国王给的。

"这是什么食物？"我想。"他们在给我吃非常小的动物！"

---

kill v. 杀死

climb v. 爬；攀登

Then I ate a lot of bread. The people watched me with wide eyes because I ate very quickly. A lot of men came with a very big cup of milk. I drank it and *called for* another cup. I drank the second cup and asked for a third cup.

"There is no more milk in the country," they showed me with their hands. But they were happy, because I ate and drank their food. They danced up and down on my body and cried, "Hekinah degull!"

After my meal, a very important person came to me. He brought a letter from the king. Servants in very fine clothes followed him. He walked up to my face and put the letter near my eyes.

Then he spoke, and often turned to the north-west. Their city and

---

然后我又吃了很多面包。这些人睁大眼睛看着我，因为我吃得很快。许多人端着非常大的一杯牛奶过来了。我喝完一杯要了一杯。喝了第二杯又要第三杯。

"这个国家没有更多的牛奶了，"他们用手给我比画。但是他们很开心，因为我吃了和喝了他们的食物。他们在我身上跳来跳去并喊叫着，"Hekinah degull！"

用完餐后，一个很重要的人来到我的面前。他带来一封来自国王的信。穿着精美衣服的仆人跟在他后面。他走到我面前，把信放在我的眼前。

然后他开始说话，并不时把头转向西北方向。他们的城市和国王在那

---

call for 要求

their king were there, about a kilometre away, I learned later.

"The king wants to see me," I understood.

I spoke to this man and showed him: "*Take* these strings *off* me."

But he moved his head: "No. We have to carry you with the strings round you. But we will give you food and drink. We will not hurt you."

I *remembered* their arrows. "I don't want to feel them again," I thought. "They can hurt me."

The great man went away. After that the people made a loud noise, and they shouted, "Peplom selan!" Then they came to my head and cut the other strings. Now I could turn my head more than before. I was happy about that.

里，离这里大约一公里远，这是我后来才知道的。

"国王想要见我，"我明白了。

我对这个人说话并且用手示意："把这些绳子拿开。"

但他摇了摇头："不，我们不得不用绳子捆着你。但是我们会给你食物和喝的东西，并且我们不会伤害你的。"

我记得他们的箭。"我可再也不想受一次了，"我想。"它们可以伤到我。"

这个大臣离开了。之后，人们发出一片吵闹声，他们喊道，"Peplom selan！"然后他们来到我的头部并割断了其他的绳子。现在我能比以前更好地转动头了。为此我很高兴。

take off　拿掉；摘掉　　　　　　　　　　　remember　v. 记得

I began to feel very tired, and I slept for about nine hours. (There was something in my food, they told me later.)

The people brought some wood and pulled me onto it. Nine hundred men worked for three hours before I was on the wood. I was *asleep*. Fifteen hundred of the king's largest horses arrived.

After four hours we began our journey. The horses pulled me on my wood, and we travelled for a long time. At night we slept. One thousand men with arrows watched me, so I stayed quiet!

The next day, at daylight, we moved again. In the *middle* of the

---

我开始觉得累了，然后睡了大约九个小时。（他们后来告诉我是食物里有东西。）

这些人带来了一些木头，然后把我拉到上面。九百个人用了三个小时才把我弄到木头上。我睡着了。国王的一千五百匹最大的马也来了。

四小时后我们开始了行程。马匹们拉着在木头上的我，我们走了很长一段时间。到了晚上我们就睡觉。一千个弓箭手看着我，所以我得保持安静！

第二天白天，我们再次行动。到了中午，我们离城市大约有一百五十

---

asleep *adj.* 睡着的   middle *n.* 中间

day, we were about 150 metres from the city. The king came out. He walked round me and looked up at me carefully.

"Do not climb up onto this man's body!" his men told him. "It is too dangerous."

We stopped *in front of* an old *church*. This was my house now! The great north door was more than a metre high and nearly a metre wide, so I could go into it on my hands. They put a string round one of my feet and tied it to the wall of the church. I could only walk about a metre away from the outside of my door.

米。国王出来迎接。他在我身边绕来绕去并仔细地抬头看着我。

"不要爬到这个人的身上！"他的侍卫们告诉他。"这太危险了。"

我们停在一个古老的教堂前面。这就是我现在的家！大北门有一米多高，近一米宽，所以我可以用手爬着进去。他们用绳子把我的一只脚绑着，绳子的另一端绑在了教堂的墙上。我只能在门外步行约一米的距离。

in front of 在……前面　　　　church n. 教堂

Chapter 2 My Life in Lilliput

Early next day I came out of my house and looked round me. To me, the country of Lilliput was *as* small *as* a garden. The tallest trees were about two metres high. I turned and looked at the city. Was this little city a picture in a child's book?

Across the road from my church, about six metres away from me, there was a very big house. I saw people on top of it. The king was there with other men, women and servants.

"They're watching me," I thought.

After a time, the king came down. He got up on his horse and

第二章 在小人国的生活

第二天一大早，我从房子里出来并环顾四周。对我来说，小人国就跟个花园一样得小。最高的树也就两米高。我转过身看着这座城市。这个小城市是小孩子书里的一张图片吗？

从我的教堂穿过马路，在离我约六米远的地方，有一个非常大的房子。我看到有人在它上面。国王与其他的男男女女还有仆人也在那里。

"他们正在看着我，"我想。

过了一段时间，国王下来了。他骑上马并走近了我。这匹马很害怕

---

as ... as 如同；像……一样

came nearer me. The horse was afraid of me, the man-mountain. It began to jump up and down. But the king — a very good *horseman* — stayed on his horse. The servants ran to the animal's head and stayed with it.

When he could, the king got down. He walked round me, but he never came too near.

Men brought me food, and the queen and her young sons watched me from the top of the house. After a time the king went away. *A number of* his men stayed and looked after me.

"Some of our people want to hurt you," they showed me with their hands. I sat on the ground near the door of my house and tried to sleep.

我，我看起来就像一个巨人山。它开始跳上跳下。但是国王——一个很好的骑手——一直骑在马身上。仆人们跑到马头跟前，站在它面前。

当马站稳的时候，国王就下了马。他绕着我走来走去，但是从来不会离得太近。

侍卫们给我带来了食物，王后和她的儿子们在屋顶上看着我。过了一会儿，国王就离开了。他的一些人留下来照看我。

"我们中有些人想伤害你，"他们用手势告诉我。我坐在大门附近的地上试图睡觉。

---

horseman *n.* 骑手

a number of 许多；一些

Suddenly, I felt arrows again and one arrow *nearly* hit my eye. The king's men caught these bad people — six men — and threw them to me.

I put five men in one hand. I took the other man and put him into my open mouth. He was very afraid. But I laughed and put the six men carefully on the ground again. They ran away from me as fast as they could!

At this time, I slept on the floor of the church or outside on the ground. But the king said to his workmen: "Make a bed for him." So they brought 600 little beds to my house and made them into one big bed.

Then the king and his great men met and *discussed* me.

突然，我又感觉到箭来了，有一支箭几乎射中我的眼睛。国王的人抓住了这些坏人———一共六个——并把他们扔给了我。

我把其中五个人放在一只手里。我把另一个人放在我张开的嘴里。他非常地害怕。但是我大笑着，并把这六个人小心地放到了地上。他们以尽可能快的速度跑走了。

这时，我睡在教堂的地板上或外面的地上。但是国王对他的工人们说："为他做一张床。"于是他们把六百张小床搬进我的房子并把他们组成一个大床。

后来国王和他的大臣会晤并讨论了我。

---

nearly *adv.* 几乎

discuss *v.* 讨论

"Perhaps he is dangerous," said the first man."We cannot *untie* his strings."

"He eats too much food," said the second man. "The people of our country will be hungry."

"Let's kill him now," said the third man. "We can do it when he is sleeping."

"No," said his friend. "What can we do with his *dead* body? It is too big."

Then a man said to the king: "Some people tried to kill this big man with their arrows, but he was kind to them. He did not hurt them."

"This is good," said the king. "We will not kill him now. But we will

---

"也许他很危险，"第一个人说。"我们不能解开绑在他身上的绳子。"

"他吃得太多了，"第二个人说。"我国的人民将会挨饿。"

"让我们现在就杀了他，"第三个人说。"在他睡觉的时候我们就可以行动。"

"不，"他的朋友说。"我们怎么处理他的尸体呢？它太大了。"

然后一个人对国王说："一些人想用他们的箭杀死这个大人，但是他对他们很友善。他并没有伤害他们。"

"好，"国王说。"我们不会杀了他。但是我们要教他我们的语

---

untie v. 解开   dead adj. 死的；失去生命的

teach him our language."

They did this, and in about three weeks I could speak quite well.

The king often came to see me and helped my teachers. We began to talk.

"Please untie these strings," I asked him.

"Not now," he answered. "But I will think about it. First — and do not be angry — my men will look at your things."

"I'll happily show your men these things," I answered, "but I'll never hurt you or your people with them."

The next day two men came and walked over me. They looked *inside* my clothes. They made *notes* on everything — my notebook,

---

言。"

　　他们这样做了，大约三个星期，我就说得很好了。

　　国王经常来看我并且帮助我的老师们一起教我。我们也开始了交谈。

　　"请解开这些绳子，"我请求他。

　　"现在不行，"他回答说。"不过我会考虑的。首先——不要生气——我的人会看看你的东西。"

　　"我会很高兴给你的人展示这些东西，"我说，"但是我绝对不会用它们伤害你和你的子民们。"

　　第二天，来了两个人在我的身体上走了个遍。他们查看了我衣服里

---

inside *adv.* 往里面　　　　　　　　note *n.* 笔记；记录

the *glasses* for my weak eyes, my money and my money-bag.

The king called to me: "Your sword is as big as five men. Please give it to me. Wait! I will bring more men."

Three thousand men stood round me and watched.

"Pull out your sword now!" shouted the king.

I took my sword from under my clothes. The sun shone on it and hurt everybody's eyes. I put it on the ground and the king's men quickly carried it away.

"Now give me those other strange things," he shouted.

I gave him my *guns*.

的东西。他们记下了所有的东西——我的笔记本，我由于视力弱而配的眼镜，我的钱和我的钱袋。

国王向我喊道："你的剑有五个人那样大。请把它给我。等一等！我带更多的人来。"

三千个男人站在我身旁，看着我。

"现在拔出你的剑吧！"国王大声喊道。

我从衣服下面拿出了我的剑。阳光照在剑上反射的光刺得大家睁不开眼。我把剑放在地上，国王的人很快把它带走了。

"现在把那些奇怪的东西给我，"他大叫着。

我给了他我的枪。

---

glasses *n.* 眼镜   gun *n.* 枪

After this, the king sent me his "*Rules*":

"*Follow* my rules and we will untie your strings," he told me.

Rules of King of Lilliput

1. The Man-Mountain will ask before he leaves our country.

2. He will ask before he comes into the city. (Two hours before this, everybody will go into their houses and stay there.)

3. He will only walk on the roads.

4. He will walk carefully. He will not put his foot on any person, or on their horses. He will not take anybody up in his hands.

之后，国王给我颁布了他的"规定"：

"如果你遵守我的规定，我们会解开你身上的绳子，"他告诉我。

由小人国的国王制定的规章条例。

1. 巨人要离开我们国家之前需要请示。

2. 在他进入城市之前需要请示。（在这之前的两小时，每个人都要进到自己的屋内。）

3. 他只能在道路上走。

4. 他要小心地走路。不能用脚踩到任何人或马。他不能用手拿任何人。

---

rule *n.* 规则；规章 　　　　follow *v.* 遵循；听从

5. He will help our ships and our men in the *war* with the people of the Island of Blefuscu.

6. He will help our workmen when they build a wall round our garden.

7. We will give him food — food for 1,728 of our people.

The reader will ask: "Why did the king use the number 1,728?" Well, I was as tall as twelve people from Lilliput. So my body was as large and as heavy as 12x12x12 people from Lilliput — 12x12 is 144; 144x12 is 1,728. This was the answer of the king's clever men. I read the rules and said to the king: "I will follow them." The next day, men came and untied the strings from my leg. Now I could walk again!

---

5. 他要帮助我们的船只及战士同不来夫斯古国的人打仗。

6. 当工人们修建花园的墙围时，他要帮助他们。

7. 我们会给他食物——这些食物可供我们1728人吃。

读者会问："为什么国王会用1728这个数字？"是的，我有来自小人国的12个人搭起来那样高。所以我的身体有12×12×12个来自小人国的人那么大和重——12×12就是144；144×12就是1728。这是国王身边聪明人的答案。我读了这些规定，并对国王说："我会遵守它们。"第二天，有人来解开了我腿上的绳子。现在我可以走动了！

---

war *n.* 战争

Chapter 3 I Make War on Blefuscu

Reldresal, a great man in Lilliput and a good friend of the king, came to my house with his servant. He wanted to speak to me. "You can put me on your hand," he said.

We talked for an hour. "There are many *problems* in Lilliput *between* the Big-enders and the Little-enders," he told me. "The king and most people are Little-enders. But the people of the Island of Blefuscu help the Big-enders here. Now there is war. Can you help us?"

"But what is this war about?" I asked. "And what is a 'Big-ender'?"

第三章 同不来夫斯古国的战争

瑞尔德里沙，小人国的一个大臣也是国王的一个好朋友，和他的仆人来到我的房子。他想和我说话。"你可以把我放在你的手上，"他说。

我们谈了一个小时。"在小人国有许多棘手的问题，主要是大端派和小端派之间的，"他告诉我。"国王和大多数人都是小端派。但是不来夫斯古国的人们帮助这里的大端派。现在这里发生了战争。你能帮助我们吗？"

"但为何要开战？"我问。"什么是'大端派'？"

---

problem *n.* 困难；难题   between *prep.* 在……之间

"It is about eggs," answered Reldresal, "and it is very important. For many years, everybody in Lilliput cut their eggs at the big end before they ate them. We were all Big-enders. But this king's grandfather cut his finger when he opened his egg. He was only a boy at the time, but his father, the king, made a new *law*. Everybody had to open their eggs at the little end. We had to be Little-enders!"

"Many of the king's people were angry and opened their eggs at the big end. Some Big-enders left our island and started new lives in Blefuscu. The Big-enders *hate* the Little-enders and the Little-enders hate the Big-enders."

I went to the king the next day. "I can help you in your war," I told

---

"那是关于鸡蛋的故事，"瑞尔德里沙回答，"这很重要。多年来，小人国的人们都在吃鸡蛋之前打破鸡蛋大的一端。我们全都是大端派。可是当今国王的祖父在打开鸡蛋时切断了他的手指。那时他还只不过是个男孩，但他的父亲，当时的国王，颁布了一项新的法律。每个人必须在小端打开鸡蛋。我们不得不成了小端派！"

"许多国王的臣民很生气，依旧在大端打开鸡蛋。一些大端派的人离开了我们的岛屿，在不来夫斯古国开始新的生活。从此，大端派同小端派互相憎恨。"

第二天我去见国王。"这场战争我可以帮助你，"我告诉他。"不来

---

law *n.* 法律   hate *v.* 厌恶；憎恨

him. "The ships of Blefuscu are waiting for the right wind. Then they will come to Lilliput. They know nothing about me because I stay away from the sea. Listen, I have a *plan*."

The king listened carefully to my words and he was very happy with my plan.

I then went to our ships and asked questions about the sea between the Island of Lilliput and the Island of Blefuscu.

"It is *not more than* a metre and a half or two metres to the bottom of the sea," they told me.

I found some very strong string. Then I left my shoes on the dry ground and walked into the water.

夫斯古国的船在等待合适的风。然后他们会来到小人国。他们对我一无所知，因为我待在远离大海的地方。听着，我有个计划。"

国王仔细地听了我的话，他对我的计划感到很高兴。

然后我来到船前，问了一些关于小人国岛和不来夫斯古岛之间的海的问题。

"这里的海深不超过一米半或两米，"他们告诉我。

我找到了一些很结实的绳子。然后我把鞋子放在干地上并走到水里。

---

plan *n.* 计划　　　　　　　　　　　　not more than 不超过

In half an hour I came to Blefuscu and saw their ships. When they saw me, a lot of men jumped out of their ships into the water.

I took my string and put it round the front of every ship. Their men sent arrows at me, and the arrows hit my hands and my face. I was afraid for my eyes, so I put on my *eye-glasses*. Then I pulled the forty largest Blefuscu ships after me through the water. And I came back to Lilliput.

The king and his great men could only see the ships from Blefuscu because only my head was above the water. But when I came nearer, I called: "I did this for the greatest King of Lilliput!"

"Thank you," the king said. "Will you go back to Blefuscu and

半小时后我来到不来夫斯古国，看到了他们的船只。当那里的人看到我时，很多人纷纷从船上跳入水中。

我拿出绳子，用它围住所有船的前端。他们向我射箭，箭射中了我的手和脸。我担心我的眼睛，所以戴上了眼镜。然后我在水里拉着不来夫斯古国最大的四十条船。然后我回到了小人国。

国王和他的大臣只能看到来自不来夫斯古国的船只，因为只有我的头在水面以上。但是当我走近了，我喊道："我这样做是为了最伟大的小人国国王！"

"谢谢你，"国王说。"你能回到不来夫斯古国把其他的船只也拿

eye-glasses *n.* 眼镜

bring the other ships? Then I will be king of their country. Its people can work for me and be my servants. I can kill the Big-enders. Then I will be king of the world."

"No, I won't help you with that," I said. "Don't kill those people — it's wrong."

He was very angry. And from that time, some of the king's friends began to talk about me *unkindly*.

"Perhaps they'll kill me now or send me away," I thought when I heard this.

About three weeks later, six important men came from Blefuscu to Lilliput. They wanted to *end* the war. They brought 500 other men with them — helpers, writers and servants.

来吗？然后我将成为他们国家的国王。它的人民可以为我工作并做我的仆人。我可以杀了大端派的人。然后我将会统治世界。"

"不，我不能帮助你，"我说。"不要杀那些人——这是错误的。"

他非常生气。从那时起，国王的一些朋友们开始不友好地谈论我。

"或许他们会杀了我或让我离开，"我听后这么想。

大约三个星期后，六个重要的人从不来夫斯古国来到小人国。他们希望结束战争。他们还带着五百个人——助手，作家和仆人。

unkindly *adv.* 不友好地　　　　　　end *v.* 结束

The King of Lilliput listened to them. Each man spoke for hours, and then the great men of Lilliput answered — with the help of about 600 men. In the end, the men from Blefuscu and the men of Lilliput wrote their names on a paper. That ended the war between their two countries.

"Don't take too much from the people of Blefuscu. They'll be unhappy again," I told the king's great men, and they listened to me.

So the King of Blefuscu was very happy. He sent me a letter — he wanted me to *visit* his country.

Do you remember the Rules of the King of Lilliput? The first Rule

小人国的国王听着他们的话。每个人都说了几个小时，然后小人国的大臣们在大约六百人的帮助下回答。最后，来自不来夫斯古国的人和小人国的人都把名字写在了一张纸上。这就结束了两国之间的战争。

"不要从不来夫斯古国的人那带走太多的东西。他们会再次不高兴的，"我告诉国王的大臣们，他们听了我的话。

于是不来夫斯古国的国王非常高兴。他寄给我一封信——他想要我去拜访他的国家。

你还记小人国王的规定吧？第一条规定："巨人离开我们国家之前需

visit *v.* 拜访

said: "The Man-Mountain will ask before he leaves the country".

I knew this rule, but I thought: "The king won't say no. I won't ask him." So I got ready for my journey.

That night, one of the king's men — a good friend — came to my house. "It is dangerous for you now in Lilliput," he told me. "The king is afraid. Perhaps you will start another war in Blefuscu and fight us from there. His men want to hurt your eyes. Then they will give you no food. You will die."

I was angry, but then I thought: "These people were very kind to me. They're not bad people, only *stupid*. I'll go to Blefuscu."

要请示。"

　　我记得这条规定，但我想："国王不会说不的。我不用问他。"所以我开始准备我的行程。

　　那天晚上，一个国王的人——我的一个好朋友，来到了我的家。"你现在在小人国很危险，"他告诉我。"国王害怕了。也许你会在不来夫斯古国开始另一场战争，在那里攻打我们。他的人想弄伤你的眼睛。然后他们不提供给你食物。你会死的。"

　　我很生气，但后来我想："这些人对我都很友好。他们不是坏人，只是愚蠢罢了。我要去不来夫斯古国。"

stupid *adj.* 愚蠢的

I took the king's largest ship. I put my clothes and my other things in it. Then I walked through the water and pulled the ship after me.

I *arrived* quickly at the Island of Blefuscu. Near the sea I met two men.

"Where's your city?" I asked them.

They showed me the way. There the King of Blefuscu and his queen came out and met me.

They wanted me to be happy. But there was no big house for me there. I had to put my coat over me and sleep outside on the ground.

我带走国王最大的船。我把我的衣服和其他的东西放在里面。然后我走进水里，把船拉在身后。

我很快就到了不来夫斯古国。我海附近我遇到了两个人。

"你们的城市在哪里？"我问他们。

他们为我带路。在那里，不来夫斯古国的国王和他的王后出来接见了我。

他们希望我高兴。但是这里没有大房子给我住。我不得不用外套裹着自己，睡在外面的地上。

---

arrive *v.* 到达

Chapter 4 I Come Home Again

Three days later, on the north-east of the island, I saw something in the sea a long way away. Perhaps it was a boat! I walked into the water and went near it. It was a boat. The wind and water *pushed* it and turned it over in the water.

I ran back to the city. "Can you send 20 large ships and 2,000 men?" I asked the king. "I want to bring the boat back to the beach."

The king's ships came. They tied strings round the boat and pulled it nearer the island. Then I took it and turned it over the right way. It was fine.

第四章 再次回家

三天以后，在岛的东北部，我看到在海面上很远的地方有什么东西。也许那是一条船！我走到水里并向它走近。这是一条船。风和水推着它并把它掀翻在了水里。

我跑回到城市里。"你能派出二十艘大船和两千个人吗？"我问国王。"我想把小船拉回到海滩。"

国王的船来了。他们在船的周围系上绳子并把它拉到了离岛较近的地方。然后我把它翻过来。它完好无损。

push *v.* 推

"Now I can go back to my country," I cried.

"I do not want you to go," said the king.

But he gave me food and men. The men helped me, and after two or three days I was ready. I took six animals with me because I wanted to show them in my country. I wanted to take some little people too, but they were *afraid*.

I left the Island of Blefuscu on 1st May, 1702. On my third day at sea, I saw a ship. I called to her, but nobody answered. Then the ship came nearer and her men saw me. It was an English ship!

I was very happy to see it. I carried my things onto it — I put the

---

"现在我可以回到我的国家了，"我喊着。

"我不想让你走，"国王说。

但他还是给了我食物和人。那些人帮助我，两三天后我就准备好了。我随身带了六只小动物，因为我想在我的国家展示它们。我也想带一些小人，但是他们很害怕。

我于1702年5月1日离开了不来夫斯古国。第三天我在海上看到了一艘船。我对着它大声呼喊，但没有人回答。然后船越来越近最后上面的人看到了我。这是一艘英国船！

我很高兴看到它。我把我的东西搬了上去——把六只动物放在我的帽

---

afraid *adj.* 害怕的

six animals in my hat!

One man on the ship was an old friend, Peter Williams. He told the other men my name and everybody was very kind to me.

"Where are you travelling from?" they asked.

I talked about my *journeys*, and they said: "These things can't be true. You're ill from your travels."

So I brought out the little animals and showed the men on the ship. Everybody looked at them with wide eyes. "Your story is true!" they laughed.

I will not tell the reader about that journey, because nothing really happened. One of my animals died, but I sold the other animals in England for a lot of money.

子里！

　　船上有一个男人是我的一个老朋友，彼得·威廉姆斯。他告诉了其他人我的名字，大家都对我很好。

　　"你这是从哪里旅行回来的？"他们问。

　　我就说了我的旅程，他们说："这些事不可能是真的。你旅途中病了吧。"

　　于是我拿出小动物，给船上的人看。每个人都睁大眼睛看着它们。"你的故事是真的！"他们大笑着。

　　我不会告诉读者有关回家的旅程，因为真的没有什么事情发生。我的一只动物死了，但我在英国卖掉了其他的动物并赚了很多钱。

---

journey *n.* 旅程

Part 2 Gulliver in Brobdingnag

Chapter 1 I Come to Brobdingnag

I was rich after my journey to Lilliput, and I bought a house in England. "I'll live here quietly and be happy," I thought. But I could not stay there. I went to sea again.

We travelled to the Indies. We bought and *sold* things there. Near the Molucca Islands, a great wind caught us. Day after day it carried

---

第二部分　格列佛在大人国

第二章　来到大人国

我从小人国旅行回来之后就变得很富有，并在英国买了一栋房子。"我会静静地在这里幸福快乐地生活，"我想。但我不能一直待在那里。于是我再次出海。

我们前往印度群岛。我们在那里购买和出售东西。在摩鹿加群岛附近，我们遇到了强风。日复一日，强风把我们的船吹向东面。虽然我们船

---

sell *v.* 出售

our ship to the east. We had food on the ship, but after weeks in that angry wind, we had no clean water.

Then the wind died and one of the *seamen* shouted. In front of us we saw a strange country.

Men left the ship in one of the boats, and I went with them. We *looked for* water, but we could not find a river. We walked for a long time. I went south, but there was no water. So I went back to the boat.

But the boat was not there.

It was on the sea, a long way away, and the other men were in it. The boat moved very fast through the water. I opened my mouth

---

上有食物，但经过数周强风后，我们没有干净的水了。

后来风停了，一名水手大喊了起来。在我们前面，我们看到了一个奇怪的国家。

我同大家一起离开了大船上了其中一条小船。我们沿路寻找饮用水，但一条河都没能找到。我们走了很长一段时间。我去了南边，但那儿也没有水。所以我回到了船停着的地方。

但是船已经不在那里了。

它在海上，已经走远了，其他人都在船上。船在水中行驶得很快。我张大嘴想对他们大声呼喊。当我看到一个巨人在他们的船边时，我就不再

---

seaman *n.* 水手

look for 寻找

because I wanted to shout to them. Then I stopped when I saw a very big man near their boat. The sea was only half-way up his legs!

I turned and ran away to the mountains. I was afraid for my life.

After a time, I found a very wide road through some trees. I walked on it and looked round me.

"These aren't trees," I thought." It's *corn*, about twelve metres high, I think. And this isn't a road. It's a way through the corn."

I heard a loud noise and I was afraid again. Suddenly I saw seven big men next to me.

"They're cutting the corn!" I cried. "They'll cut me too and I'll die here, away from my dear *wife* and children!"

喊了。海的深度才到他腿的一半。

我转过身跑到了山上。我担心自己的性命。

过了一会儿，我发现了一些树中间有一条非常宽阔的路。我走在这条路上并打量着四周。

"这些不是树，"我心想。"是玉米，我想大约十二米高。这也不是一条路。而是一条穿过玉米地的通道。"

我听见一声巨响，再一次害怕了。突然，我看到在我身旁有七个巨人。

"他们正在割玉米！"我喊着。"他们也会把我给割了，我就要远离我亲爱的妻子和孩子死在这里了！"

---

corn *n.* 玉米   wife *n.* 妻子

A man heard me and looked round. Then this big man saw me in the corn. He walked to me and I began to shout loudly: "His foot is going to kill me!"

The man stopped. For a minute he looked down at me carefully. (We look at a small animal in the same way, and think: "Will it hurt me?") Then he took me up in his *fingers* and put me about three metres from his eyes. I was about twenty metres from the ground, so I was afraid.

"Perhaps he'll throw me down onto the ground and put his foot on me," I thought. "In our country, we sometimes do that to animals."

I put my hands up. I wanted to say, "Please don't kill me!" and "Your fingers are hurting me!'

He understood. The man turned up the *bottom* of his coat and put

---

一个人听见了我的声音并环顾四周。然后这个巨人看见我在玉米地中。他向我走来，我开始大叫："他的脚会踩死我的！"

这个人突然停住了。他低头仔细地看了我一分钟。（我们也会这样看一只小动物，并想："它会伤害我吗？"）然后他把我拿起来放进手指里并放到离他眼睛约三米处。我离地面大约有二十米的距离，所以我很害怕。

"或许他会把我扔在地上并用脚来踩我，"我心想。"在我的国家，我们有时候会这样对待小动物。"

我举起双手。我想说，"请不要杀我！"和"你的手指伤到我了！"

他明白了我的意思。他卷起衣服的底部并把我放在那里。然后他把我

---

finger n. 手指

bottom n. 底部

me in there. Then he carried me to the farmer and put me back on the ground.

me in there. Then he carried me to the farmer and put me back on the ground.

I spoke to the farmer. He put me next to his ear — about two metres away — but he could not understand me. He answered me, and the noise was as loud as a lot of big guns. I could not understand his words.

The farmer carried me carefully to his house. It was time for the midday meal. His wife cried loudly when she saw me. Women in England do this when they see a *rat*. Then she began to like me.

She *cut up* some bread and meat for me. I smiled — "Thank you"— and took out my knife. Then I began to eat quickly. The

---

带到一个农夫那里，并把我放回地上。

我开始对这个农夫说话。他把我放到了耳边——大约离他的耳朵有两米——但是他听不懂我所说的话。他回答了我，声音震耳欲聋。我也听不懂他的话。

农夫把我小心翼翼地带到他家里。吃中午饭的时间到了。他的妻子看到我时就大声尖叫。英国的妇女看到一只老鼠时也会这么叫。然后她开始喜欢我了。

她把一些面包和肉切碎了给我。我笑了着说"谢谢你"——并拿出小刀。然后我开始很快地吃这些食物。这些人围着桌子——农夫和他的妻

---

rat *n.* 老鼠

cut up *切碎；剁碎*

people round the table — the farmer and his wife, three children, and the farmer's old mother — watched happily.

A cat jumped onto the table and looked down at me.

"I won't be afraid," I thought. "Then this cat won't hurt me."

I walked past the cat three or four times, and in the end she was afraid of me!

But then a worse thing happened to me. The farmer and his wife had a baby, and they showed me to this child.

He pulled my body and put my head into his open mouth. Then he *threw* me down on the floor.

I was now very tired. The farmer's wife took me to her room and put me on her bed. I slept for about two hours — in my clothes, and

子，三个孩子，以及农夫的老母亲——高兴地看着我。

一只猫也跳上了桌子，低头看着我。

"我不能害怕，"我心想。"这样这只猫就不会伤害我了。"

我在猫面前走了三四次，最后她害怕我了！

但是后来糟糕的事发生了。农夫和他的妻子有一个小孩儿，他们把我给这个小孩儿看。

他拉扯我的身体，把我的头放进他张开的嘴里。然后又把我摔在地板上。

我现在很累。农夫的妻子带我到她的房间，把我放在了床上。我睡了

throw *v.* 扔；投

with my sword.

When I woke up, I looked round me. The room was very big — about 100 metres wide and 60 metres high — and the bed was nearly 20 metres wide and about 8 metres from the floor.

Suddenly I sat up, afraid. Two rats were on the bed. They wanted some meat — me! One rat came near me, and I pulled out my sword. The two animals were not afraid. One rat tried to eat my arm, and I cut its *stomach* with my sword. It died. I could not kill the other rat, but I cut its back.

The farmer's daughter helped me. She was about nine years old and about twelve metres high. But in other ways she was not different from an English girl of the same age. She played with a

---

大约两个小时——穿着衣服，随身带着我的剑。

当我醒来时，我四周看了看。这间屋子很大——约一百米宽，六十米高——床近二十米宽，离地约八米高。

突然我坐起来，害怕了。床上有两只老鼠。他们想要一些肉——那就是我！一只老鼠过来靠近我，我拔出了剑。这两只动物都不害怕。一只老鼠试图吃我的手臂，我用剑砍到了它的胃。它死了。我没能杀死另一只老鼠，但我把它的背砍伤了。

农夫的女儿帮助了我。她大约九岁，有十二米那么高。但在其他方面，她与同年龄的英国女孩没有什么不同。她在她的卧室里玩着一个小房

---

stomach *n.* 胃

small house in her bedroom and I slept in the little house away from the rats and other animals.

The farmer's daughter was also my teacher. I showed her things and she told me the words for them. So in one or two days I could ask for everything. She called me Grildrig. Then her family used that name, and later everybody in their country — Brobdingnag — called me Grildrig. It means a very small man.

The girl *looked after* me every minute of every day and night. I called her my glumdalclitch, my little helper. But in the end I made her very unhappy.

People in the villages near the farmer heard about me and discussed me.

"This animal," they said, "is only as big as a splacknuck! (This

---

子，而我睡在这个远离老鼠和其他动物的小房子里。

农夫的女儿也是我的老师。我给她看我的东西，她教我他们的语言。所以一两天的时间我就可以要想要的东西了。她叫我格里尔特里格。然后她的家人也开始用这个名字，后来在他们国家——大人国——所有人都叫我格里尔特里格。它的意思就是一个很小的人。

这个女孩日日夜夜每时每刻都照看我。我称她为我的葛兰朵克丽琪，我的小帮手。但是最后我让她很不高兴。

农夫家附近的村子里的人们听说了我并一起讨论我。

"这只动物，"他们说，"只有一个splacknuck那么大！（splacknuck是一种在他们的国家低于两米的动物。）但在其他方面，它和一个很小的人

---

look after 照顾

was an animal in their country under two metres long.) But in other ways it is not different from a very small man."

"It speaks its language, and it is learning our words. It walks on two legs, but its legs are very small and weak. It wears clothes, and it has a very small sword."

The head man of the village came to the farmer's house because he wanted to see me. I stood on the table and spoke to him. Then the *visitor* talked to the farmer about me for a long time. Glumdalclitch listened, but she was more and more unhappy. Later, she cried and told me: "They have a plan. They want to show you to the people of our town when they sell the corn there. Some people will put you in their hands. Perhaps they will hurt you when they do this. My father will *make money*, but I will try to stop him."

没有什么不同。"

　　"它使用它的语言，并且也在学习我们的语言。它用两条腿走路，但它的腿很弱小。它穿着衣服，并且随身携带一把非常小的剑。"

　　这个村的村长来到农夫家里，因为他想要见我。我站在桌子上和他说话。然后这位访客和农夫谈了很长一段时间关于我的事。葛兰朵克丽琪在一旁听着，但她越来越不开心。后来，她哭着告诉我："他们有一个计划。他们想在出售玉米的时候让镇上的人来看你。有人会把你拿在手里。他们这样做时也许会伤害到你。我的父亲将以此来赚钱，但我会尽力阻止他的。"

---

visitor n. 访客；游客　　　　　　　　　make money 赚钱

But she could not stop her father. One day he took me to the nearest town. His workmen made a box for me, with a little door in it. He carried me in this on his horse, and his daughter sat behind him. I had a very bad journey. The horse moved up and down as quickly as a ship in an angry wind.

The town was only forty kilometres away, about half an hour's journey. But I was tired when I arrived. Then the farmer *found* a room and showed me on a table to about thirty people every time.

Glumdalclitch stood on a chair next to the table and helped me. She asked me questions. I knew the answers now.

但是她阻止不了她的父亲。有一天他带我去了最近的镇里。他的工人为我做了一个盒子，上面有一扇小门。他把我装在里面，然后就上了马，他的女儿坐在他身后。这一路对我来说非常糟糕。马上下颠簸，就像狂风中的一条船一样。

这个镇仅有四十公里远，约半小时的路程。但是到达那里的时候，我累坏了。然后农夫找了一个房间，并把我放在桌子上，一次让三十个人来观看。

葛兰朵克丽琪站在桌子旁边的椅子上帮我。她问了我一些问题。现在我知道答案了。

find *v.* 找到

"What is your name?" she asked in the language of Brobdingnag.

"My name," I said in the same language, "is Lemuel Gulliver." I *had to* shout.

"Where do you come from?"

"I come from England."

"Why are you very small?"

"I am not small. I am as big as the other men in England. You and your people are very, very big."

The people laughed then. The loud noise hurt my ears and made me ill. Then I had to walk on the table and drink. I pulled out my

---

"你叫什么名字？"她用大人国的语言问。

"我的名字，"我用他们的语言说，"是列缪尔·格列佛。"我必须大声喊着。

"你来自哪里？"

"我是从英国来的。"

"你为什么很小？"

"其实我不小，在英国我跟其他人一样大。你和你们国家的人是非常非常的大树。"

然后人们大笑了起来。这种巨大的吵闹声伤了我的耳朵，我生病了。

---

have to 不得不；必须

sword and showed them an English *swordfight*.

And I had to do a lot of other things.

The farmer showed me twelve times that day. After that, and after a very bad journey back to the farmer's house, I was very tired and ill. I did not get better. The farmer wanted more and more money. He began to show me every day at his farm, and people came from a long way away.

Glumdalclitch cried because I was very weak.

"What can I do?" she said.

然后我不得不在桌子上走来走去并喝着东西。我拿出我的剑给他们表演了英国击剑。

同样，我还不得不做很多其他的事。

那天农夫把我展示了十二次。在那之后，我又经历了十分糟糕的旅程。回到农夫家中，我累得病了。我的病情没有好转。农夫希望有越来越多的钱。他开始在他的农场里每天都展示我，观看的人都是从很远的地方来的。

葛兰朵克丽琪因为我很虚弱而哭了。

"我能做点什么呢？"她说。

---

swordfight *n.* 击剑

Chapter 2 I Meet the King and Queen

I was very ill now.

"I think he is going to die," said the farmer. "I will show him more before he dies. Then I can make more money."

He began to show me in the big cities. The first was Lorbrulgrud, the greatest city in Brobdingnag. The king lived there. He wanted the farmer to show me to the queen.

"Perhaps the queen will help me," I thought.

The queen asked me some questions about my country and my *travels*, and I answered them.

第二章 拜见国王和王后

我现在病得很厉害。

"我想他快要死了，"农民说。"我会在他死之前更多地展示他。这样我就能赚更多的钱了。"

他开始在一些大城市里展示我。第一个是洛布鲁格鲁德城，大人国最大的城市。国王就住在那里。他想要农夫把我展示给王后。

"或许王后会帮助我，"我心想。

王后问了我一些关于我的国家和我的旅行的问题，我回答了他们。

travel *n.* 旅行

"Would you like to live here?" she asked me in her language.

"Yes," I answered, "but I work for the farmer. I'm his servant. I'll have to stay with him."

"Perhaps he will sell you to me," the queen answered.

The queen bought me from the farmer for a lot of money.

"Can his daughter work for you?" I asked the queen. "She's a good friend. I don't want to leave her."

Glumdalclitch came with me and we were very happy.

One day, the queen took me to the king. He was very *busy* with his books and papers. He looked at me on his wife's hand, but only

---

"你愿意住在这里吗？"她用她的语言问我。

"是的，"我回答，"但是我为这个农夫工作。我是他的仆人。我不得不和他待在一起。"

"也许他会把你卖给我，"王后说。

王后用很大一笔钱从农夫那里把我买了下来。

"他的女儿能为您工作吗？"我问王后。"她是我一个很好的朋友。我不想离开她。"

于是葛兰朵克丽琪和我一起过来，我们很快乐。

有一天，王后带我去见国王。他正忙于他的书籍和文件。他看到我在

---

busy *adj.* 忙碌的

quickly.

The queen laughed with him and put me in front of the king. He asked me some questions and I told him my name and about my travels.

He *sent for* his men. They watched me, and they talked about me for hours. Then they spoke to the king.

"This thing," they said, "is not an animal. It cannot fly or run very fast. It cannot climb trees, or run away under the ground. It is not a very small person because it is smaller than the smallest person in the world. It is a Thing — and nobody planned this Thing. It is a *Mistake*."

他妻子的手上只是轻轻一瞥。

王后跟国王一起大笑起来，并把我放到国王的面前。他问了我一些问题，我告诉了他我的名字和我的旅行。

他召唤来他的大臣们。他们看着我，就我谈论了好几个小时。然后，他们开始对国王说话。

"这个东西，"他们说，"不是动物。它不会飞也不会跑得很快。它不能爬树，也不能在地下跑。它不是一个很小的人，因为它比世界上最小的人还要小。它是某种东西——没有人设计它。它的出现就是个错误。"

---

send for 请某人来   mistake *n.* 错误

I spoke to the king.

"I'm not a Thing," I said. "In my country there are millions of men and women of my size. The animals, trees and houses are the right size for us. We have our language, our *ruler* and our laws."

I told him about England and the other countries of Europe. He listened carefully. Then he sent his men away.

"I want to hear more from this little man," he told the queen. "Build a house for him."

The queen sent for the best *woodworker* in the country and he made a box for me. He was a very good worker, and in three weeks I

我开始对国王说话。

"我不是一件东西，"我说。"在我的国家，有数百万跟我一样大小的男人和女人。动物，树木和房屋的大小适合我们。我们有自己的语言、统治者和法律。"

我告诉他关于英国以及欧洲其他国家的一些情况。他仔细地听着。然后他让大臣们离开了。

"我想从这个小人那儿听到更多的东西，"他告诉王后。"给他建造一个房子吧。"

王后派了大人国里最好的木工，他为我做了一个盒子。他是一个很好

---

ruler *n.* 统治者   woodworker *n.* 木工

had a big room. It was about five metres long, five metres wide, and three metres high. It had two windows and a door. Glumdalclitch could open the top and clean the room. She took my bed out in the morning and put it in at night.

The queen liked me very much. At dinner time I sat at my table on her dinner table. The queen always cut my food as small as she could. Then I cut it again with my knife and ate it slowly.

On Wednesdays nobody worked, and every Wednesday the king had dinner with his family. Then the king liked to have me and my table near him. He asked me questions about Europe and its people, its laws and *ideas*, and its rulers.

的工人，在三个星期内，我就有了一个大屋子。它长五米，宽五米，高三米。它有两扇窗户和一扇门。葛兰朵克丽琪可以打开顶部来打扫房间。她早上把我的床拿出来，晚上把它又放回去。

王后非常喜欢我。在吃饭的时候，我的桌子就在她用餐的桌子上。王后总是尽可能把我的食物切小。然后我把它再用我的刀子切小并慢慢地吃下去。

在星期三的时候，没有人工作，而且每当星期三国王就同他的家人一起用餐。国王喜欢把我和我的桌子放在他旁边。他会问我一些关于欧洲和欧洲人的问题，例如法律和思想，还有统治者。

---

idea *n.* 思想

I spoke to him about our wars, our great rich families, the fights between our *churchmen*, our rulers and *Parliament*. The king laughed and made a loud noise.

He said to the queen: "Now we know that we are stupid! We think we are important people. But these funny little people think they are important. Perhaps they build a lot of houses in the same place and call them cities. Perhaps they fight, and say bad things about one friend to another friend. Perhaps they are not very different from other people."

Of course I was angry.

"How can he say these things about England?" I thought. "England is a good and great country. We win wars."

我对他讲我们的战争，我们的富有家族，我们不同教徒间的斗争，我们的统治者和议会。国王大笑着，并弄出很大的声音。

他对王后说："现在我们知道我们是愚蠢的！我们认为我们是重要的人。但这些可笑的小人认为他们是重要的。也许他们在同一个地方建造了很多房子，然后把它们叫作城市。也许他们打仗，对另外一个朋友说一个朋友的坏话。也许他们跟其他人没有什么不同。"

当然，我听了很生气。

"他怎么能这么说英国呢？"我心想。"英国是一个很好的很伟大的国家。我们赢得了很多战争。"

---

churchman *n.* 教徒   Parliament *n.* 议会

"Was I right when I was angry? To me, these people were not big and *ugly* and noisy now. Perhaps I will *laugh at* the people in my country when I see them again."

The king was very interested. He often asked for me. I had to talk about my country, and I did that happily.

"My country," I told him, "is really three great countries under one great ruler. The three countries are in two islands, but we also have places in America."

"But there were people in America before the Europeans went there," he said. "Why don't these people have an American ruler?"

I tried to tell him the answer to this, but he could not understand.

"我生气对吗？对我来说，这些人现在不大了，也不丑陋和喧闹了。也许当我再看到我们国家的人的时候，我也会嘲笑他们。"

国王非常地感兴趣。他经常问我问题。我不得不谈谈我的国家，并且那样做我很开心。

"我的国家，"我告诉他，"实际上是在一个伟大的统治者统治下的三个大国。这三个国家在两个岛屿上，但是我们也有一些地方在美洲。"

"但是在欧洲人去之前美洲就有人了，"他说。"为什么这些人没有一个美洲的统治者呢？"

我尽力告诉他这个问题的答案，但是他不能理解。

---

ugly *adj.* 丑陋的 　　　　　　　　　　　　　　　　　　　　laugh at 嘲笑

Then I told him about our English Parliament.

"It makes the laws for our country," I said. "There are two *Houses* in this Parliament. One is the House of Lords. Some great families have a place in this House. A father gives this place to his son when he dies. The House of Lords helps the king or queen. It discusses the laws from the other House, the House of Commons."

The king had more questions. "How do these men learn about the laws?" he asked. "It is difficult work."

"They have to know that the law is good for the country — not for them. Do they learn these things when they are boys, or young men?"

然后我告诉他关于我们英国议会的一些事情。

"它为我们国家制定法律，"我说。"在议会里有两个议院。一个是上议院。一些尊贵的家族都会在这个议院里有一席之位。父亲死后会把席位留给儿子。上议院来协助国王或王后。它会讨论下议院制定的法律。"

国王会问更多的问题。"这些人是怎样学习法律的？"他问。"这是艰难的工作。"

"他们需要知道法律对国家是有益的——而不是对他们。当他们还是孩子或轻年的时候，他们就学习这些东西吗？"

House *n.* 议院；机构

"No," I answered."They learn when they go to the House of Lords. Before that, they learn to kill animals, and they learn to fight. "

"The House of Commons is very different. The people of the country send men to it, and those men speak for them. Nobody pays them, but they want to help people. "

"A new law first *goes through* the House of Commons. Then the House of Lords discusses it. Sometimes, the ruler wants more money from the people, and then he has to ask the House of Commons."

"How can the men in the House of Commons do this work for no money?" the king asked again and again. "Perhaps some men are

---

"不，"我回答。"当他们进到上议院里面时才开始学的。在那之前，他们学习猎杀动物，学习打仗。"

"下议院是非常不同的。国家的百姓派遣代表进到里面，这些人是为他们说话的。没有人会付费给他们，但是他们想帮助百姓。"

"一项新的法律先通过下议院。然后，上议院再进行讨论。有时，统治者想向人们要更多钱，那么他就不得不向下议院询问。"

"下议院的人是如何做这项没有钱的工作的？"国王一遍又一遍地问。"也许有些人是坏的！也许他们制定一项法律时会从百姓手中拿钱。

---

go through 通过

bad! Perhaps they take money from people when they make a law. Perhaps they get more money from the people for the ruler or his friends."

He did not understand my answers, so I told him other things about my country.

"I do not like," he said, "to hear about wars. They *cost* your country a lot of money. Perhaps, my little Grildrig, you are now better than your little people because you know other places in the world. You are a good man — but sometimes stupid because, of course, your head is very small."

I was angry. "We are small people with small heads," I thought, "but we know a lot of things in our country. I'll tell him about *gunpowder*."

也许他们为了统治者或者朋友而从百姓手中拿钱。"

他不明白我的回答，所以我告诉他关于我们国家的其他一些事。

"我不喜欢，"他说，"听到战争。它们会花费国家很多的钱。也许，我的小格里尔特里格，你现在是比你们那些小人要更好，因为你知道世界上的其他地方。你是一个好人——但有时愚蠢，因为，当然了，你的头很小。"

我很生气。"我们是有着小头的小人，"我想，"但我们知道很多我们国家的事情。我会告诉他关于火药的事。"

---

cost *v.* 花费　　　　　　　　　　　gunpowder *n.* 火药

"We have very clever men in my country," I began. "They can make a dangerous *powder*. They put this powder into a long gun. Inside the gun there is a very hard ball. When you put fire near the powder, there's a loud noise. The powder pushes the ball from the gun, and the ball flies out very fast. When it hits something, it breaks it."

"A ball from the biggest gun will kill a lot of men. Or it will break the strongest wall, or send the biggest ship to the bottom of the sea."

"Who can make this powder?" the king asked me.

"A lot of people, from good schools," I said. "I can make it. I can show your workmen and they can make big guns — perhaps sixty

---

"在我的国家我们有非常聪明的人，"我开始说了。"他们能制造出一种危险的粉末。他们把这种粉末装在一个长枪里。在枪里面有一个很硬的球。当你让火接近粉末时，就会发出一个响亮的声音。这种粉末就会把球从枪里推出去，并且球很快地飞出去。当它撞到东西时，就会把它毁坏。

"从最大的枪里出来的球会杀死很多的人。或将打破最坚固的墙，或把最大的船击沉到海底。"

"谁会做这种粉末？"国王问我。

"很多来自好学校的人，"我说。"我就能做。我可以告诉你的工人们并能让他们做出大枪——大概有六十米长。有了二十把或三十把这样的

---

powder *n.* 粉末

metres long. With twenty or thirty of these guns, you can break down the walls of the strongest town in your country in hours."

"Stop!" the king said. "Never speak of these things again! Don't talk about them to me or to anybody in my country. Or you will die!"

"This is strange!" I thought. "He is a good king, and he understands a lot of things. But sometimes people want *changes* — and he doesn't want to hurt anybody! What will he do when they don't want a king here?"

"Your rulers, your men in Parliament and your clever men are not working for the people of your country," said the king. "A good farmer, with his fruit or *vegetables*, helps his people better than them."

枪，你就可以在几小时之内打破你们国家最坚固的城墙。"

"停！"国王说。"不要谈论这些东西了！不要把它们说给我或是我们国家的任何人。否则你会死的！"

"这就奇怪了！"我心想。"他是一个好国王，他知道很多东西。但有时人们想要改变——他不想伤害任何人！如果人们不想要国王的时候，他会做什么呢？"

"你们的统治者，你们在议会里的人和你们那些聪明的人不是在为国家的百姓而工作，"国王说。"一个好的农夫，只要有水果或蔬菜，就能比他们更好地帮助人民。"

---

change *n.* 改变   vegetable *n.* 蔬菜

Chapter 3 I Come Home Again

After two years in the country of Brobdingnag, the king and queen made a journey to the towns and cities of the south. I travelled with them in my box.

We arrived near the sea. Glumdalclitch and I were very *tired* after our journey, but I wanted to see the sea again.

"Glumdalclitch," I said, "we're tired, but I'd like to be outside. Let's go to the sea."

She called a boy. He carried my box, and we went out. The boy

---

第三章 再次回家

在大人国生活了两年后，国王和王后去了南部的小镇和城市旅行。我在我的盒子里跟他们一起旅行。

我们来到了大海附近。结束旅程后，葛兰朵克丽琪和我都很累，但我想再去看看海。

"葛兰朵克丽琪，"我说，"虽然我们很累，但是我想出去。我们去海边吧。"

她叫了一个男孩。他带着我的盒子，我们就出去了。这个男孩很不小

---

tired *adj.* 疲惫的

was not very careful. I felt more ill than before.

"I'll sleep for a time," I told Glumdalclitch.

She shut my windows and my door. Then I went to sleep.

Suddenly I woke up, because the box moved. Up and up, and very fast. I moved to a window and opened it. I looked out, but I could see nothing — only sky.

Then I knew.

"One of the country's great *seabirds* is carrying me away!" I cried. "When it's near its home, it will break my box. Then the bird will carry me to the young birds for food."

My box began to move faster and faster — up and down.

心。我觉得身体比以前更加糟糕了。

"我要睡一会儿，"我告诉葛兰朵克丽琪。

她关上了窗户和门。然后我就睡觉了。

我突然醒来，因为箱子在移动。越来越高，并且速度很快。我移到窗前，并把窗子打开。我向外看着，但什么也没看到——只有天空。

然后我就明白了。

"这个国家的一只大海鸟把我带走了！"我大声喊道。"当它接近它的家时，它就会打破我的盒子。然后这只鸟会让我成为小鸟们的食物。"

我的盒子移动得越来越快了——上下颠簸。透过窗户我看见另外两只

---

seabird *n.* 海鸟

Through the window I saw two other birds. They began to fight with my bird and it could not carry me.

I fell into the sea with a loud noise and I went down…down…under the dark water. Then, suddenly, my box came up again to the top of the water and stayed there.

"I'm not dead!" I cried, "and the water isn't coming in. But what's going to happen to me? How can I *get out*? Will I die because I'm hungry or thirsty or cold? Will great winds break my box?"

One day, I heard a loud noise. Something pulled my box up about a metre, and I could hear the sound of people. So I shouted in different languages. Something or somebody moved the top of the box, and then I heard, in English, the words: "Is anybody there?"

鸟。它们开始攻击抓我的鸟，因此它抓不住我了。

随着一声巨响我就掉进了海里，一直下沉……下沉……沉到黑暗的水中。然后，突然，我的盒子又浮到水面上漂着。

"我还没死！"我大声喊着，"水没有进来。但将会发生什么？我怎么才能出去？我会因为饥饿，口渴或寒冷而死吗？大风会不会弄坏我的盒子？"

有一天，我听到一声巨响。有东西把我的盒子拉高了大约一米，我能听到有人说话。所以我用不同的语言大声喊叫着。有什么东西或者人搬开了盒子的顶部，然后我听到有人用英语说："有人吗？"

---

get out 出去

"Yes," I shouted." I'm an *Englishman*. Please help me."

"Your box is now near our ship," he answered, "and one of our men is going to break it. Then you can climb out."

"No don't, wait!" I called. "Pull the box out of the water and put me on a table."

The men laughed. When I was out of the box and in the ship, I understood. They were not bigger than I was!

"Why are you shouting?" asked one man.

"Do you know the country of Brobdingnag?" I asked him. "There the people are very, very big — more than twenty metres tall. I had

"是的，"我喊道。"我是一个英国人。请帮帮我。"

"你的盒子现在离我们的船很近，"他说，"我们中会有人去打破它。然后你就可以爬出来了。"

"不不，等一下！"我喊着。"把盒子拉出水面，把我放在桌子上吧。"

人们都笑了。当我从盒子里出来站在船上时，我明白了。他们并不比我大！

"你为什么大喊大叫？"一个男人问。

"你知道大人国吗？"我问他。"那里的人非常非常的大——比二十

Englishman *n.* 英国人

to shout, or they couldn't hear me. I was there before my journey in the box."

"This can't be true," he said.

So I showed him the things in my box. When he saw a tooth from one of the king's servants, he laughed. It was *nearly* half a metre long.

"Please can I have it?" he asked.

After that he was kind to me. "When you're in England again, you'll have to write down your story," he said.

米还要高。我不得不大喊，否则他们听不到我的。我在盒子里的旅程之前我是在那里的。"

"这不可能是真的，"他说。

于是我就给他展示了我盒子里的东西。当他看到一个国王的仆人的一颗牙齿时，他笑了。它几乎有半米长。

"你能把它给我吗？"他问。

从那之后，他对我很好。"当你再到英国时，你得把你的故事写下来，"他说。

---

nearly adv. 几乎

Then I travelled home to my family. It was *strange* in a world with people of my size.

"Am I in Lilliput again?" I thought.

I could not see my wife and children because I always looked up at the sky. I had to do this in Brobdingnag when I wanted to see people's faces.

My family and friends talked about me.

"He's ill after his travels," said one friend.

"He isn't going to sea again!" said my wife.

But I travelled again, and you will read about that journey in my next story.

然后我就回到了家。在所有人都跟我一样大小的这个世界里我感到有点陌生。

"我又在小人国了吗？"我心想。

我看不见我的妻子和孩子，因为我总是仰望天空。当我在大人国想看到人们的脸时，我不得不这样做。

我的家人和朋友们开始谈论我。

"他在旅行回来后就病了，"一位朋友说。

"他不会再出海啦！"我的妻子说。

但我再一次出发了，你会在我的下一个故事里读到那段旅程。

---

strange *adj.* 陌生的

Part 3 Gulliver in the Country of the Houyhnhnms

Chapter 1 Houyhnhnms and Yahoos

I stayed in England with my family for some months, but then I wanted to travel again. I left England in my ship in September 1710. For a month we had a good wind. Then it died and we could not move. The seamen were all ill.

"I have to find more men," I thought. "I'll go to the *island* of Barbados."

第三部分 格列佛在慧骃国

第一章 "慧骃"和"野胡"

我和我的家人在英国待了几个月，但后来我又想旅行了。我于1710年9月乘船离开了英国。海上有一个月风都对我们很有利。后来风停了，我们不能航行了。水手们全都病了。

"我必须找到更多的人，"我想。"我要去巴巴多斯岛。"

---

island *n.* 岛

There I found men, but the idea was a mistake. These men, and mine, took the ship. They put me in a small room and *tied* me to my bed.

"There's a man outside your door," they said. "Don't come out or he'll kill you. We have your ship now. So we can fight other ships and take things from them."

They brought me food and drink and I stayed in that room for a long time.

Then, one day, a great wind took the ship out of our way. In May 1711 the other men saw a *beach*, and they took me to it in the ship's small boat.

"What country is this?" I asked them. They said nothing and left me there.

在那里我找到了些人，但这是个错误的想法。这些人伙同我的人抢了船。他们把我关在一个小房间里，并把我绑在床上。

"有人在你门外面，"他们说。"别出来，否则他会杀了你。我们现在控制着你的船。所以我们可以攻打其他的船，并从他们那里抢东西。"

他们给我带来了食物和喝的，我在房间里待了很长一段时间。

后来，有一天，一场强风改变了船的航向。那是1711年5月，其他人看到了一个海滩，他们用船上的小船把我带到了那里。

"这是什么地方？"我问他们。他们什么都没说就把我留在了那儿。

---

tie *v.* 系   beach *n.* 海滩

I began to walk away from the sea. I had my sword with me, and I was happy about that.

When I came to a road, I walked carefully. I was afraid of arrows. I saw some animals near the road, and other animals up in the trees. They were very dirty and very ugly. The bigger animals had a lot of hair on their heads, their faces and their backs, and on the front of their legs and feet. The smaller animals had longer hair on their heads but not much hair on their bodies. Their hair was different colours — brown, red, black and yellow.

I hated these animals. When I looked at them, I felt *sick*.

I walked again. "Perhaps I will meet some men and they'll help me," I thought.

我开始步行离开大海。我随身携带着我的剑，为此我很高兴。

当我来到一条大路上，我就小心地走着。我害怕被箭射中。我看到了一些动物在路边，还有动物在树上。它们非常肮脏也非常丑陋。较大的动物的头上、脸和背上、腿和脚的前面都有很多的毛发。较小动物们的头上也有较长的毛发，但其他身体部位没有太多毛发。他们的毛发五颜六色——有棕色、红色、黑色和黄色。

我讨厌这些动物。当我看着他们时，我就想吐。

我继续往前走。"也许我会遇见一些人，他们会帮助我的，"我想。

---

sick *adj.* 想呕吐；恶心

Suddenly, I met one of these ugly animals on the road. He stopped and looked hard at me. This made his face uglier. He put out his front foot and I hit him with my sword.

"You will not hurt me, you ugly animal!" I cried.

I did not want to hurt him too much. But he made a loud noise and about forty more animals ran to him. They shouted at me and made angry noises.

I moved to a tree and stood with my back to it. I used my sword, but some animals climbed up the tree. From there they threw things down at me.

Suddenly the animals all ran away *quickly*. I left the tree and started on the road again.

突然，我在路上遇到了其中一个丑陋的动物。他停下来，冷酷地望着我。这使他的脸更加的丑陋。他伸出前脚，我就用我的剑刺他。

"你伤害不到我的，你这个丑陋的动物！"我大声喊着。

我并不想使劲儿地伤害他。但他发出了一个响亮的声音，然后约有四十多只动物向他跑来。他们冲我喊叫，发出很愤怒的声音。

我走向一棵树并背靠着它。我挥舞着我的剑，但有些动物爬上了树。他们从那里扔下东西来砸我。

突然，所有的动物很快地逃走了。于是我离开了树，重新上路。

---

quickly *adv.* 迅速地

MCGRAW-HILL

"Why are they so afraid?" I thought.

Then I saw the answer to my question.

It was a horse. He saw me and stopped in front of me. Then this horse looked carefully at my face and hands and feet. He walked round and round me. I tried to walk away but he stopped again in front of me.

I put my hand on his back. We do this in England when we meet a strange horse. But this horse did not like it. He put up his left front foot and *pushed away* my hand! Then he made the sounds of a horse, again and again. But each sound was different.

"Is he speaking a language?" I thought.

"他们为什么这么害怕？"我想。

然后我就看到了答案。

这是一匹马。他看到我就停在了我面前。然后这匹马仔细地看着我的脸、手和脚。他在我身边绕来绕去。我试图走开，但他又停了下来站在我的面前。

我把我的手放在他的背部。在英国遇到一匹陌生的马时，我们就是这样做的。但是这匹马不喜欢这样。他抬起了他的左前蹄，推开了我的手！然后他一遍又一遍发出叫声。但每个声音都不同。

"他在说话？"我心想。

---

push away 推开

Another horse arrived, and the two horses made noises.

"They're having a *conversation*," I thought.

I was a little afraid and I began to walk away. But the first horse, a grey horse, made a sound. I understood — he wanted me to stop. The two horses came near me and looked carefully at my face and hands. The grey horse moved my hat with his right foot and it fell to the ground. I put it on again. The other horse — a brown horse — felt my coat, then my clothes.

He hurt me and I shouted loudly: "I'm an Englishman. Please can I sit on your back and go to a town or village?"

The two horses began to talk about me again in their horse-

另一匹马来了，然后这两匹马一起叫着。

"他们正在交谈，"我想。

我有点害怕于是就走开了。但第一匹马，一匹灰色的马，叫了一声。我明白了——他想让我停下来。这两匹马走近我，认真地看着我的脸和手。灰色的马用他的右蹄动了下我的帽子，它掉到了地上。我再次把它戴上。另一匹马——一匹棕色的马——碰碰我的外套和我的衣服。

他伤到了我，于是我大声喊："我是英国人。请问我能坐在你的背上去一个城镇或乡村吗？"

这两匹马再次开始用他们的马语谈论我。其中有一个词的发音是

---

conversation *n.* 交谈

language. One word made the sound Yahoo. I tried to say it too. Then I said it to the horses.

The grey horse said the word again and again. I repeated it, but not very well. The brown horse gave me a second word, a more *difficult* one: Houyhnhnm. I tried it two or three times. The last time was better.

One horse talked to the other horse — about me, I think — and the brown horse went away. The grey horse told me: "I walk in the front !" So I followed him. Sometimes I walked too slowly and he cried, "Hhuun, Hhuun."

"I'm tired and I can't walk faster," I showed him. "Can I sit on the ground?"

Yahoo。我也想试着说这个词。然后我就对这些马说了。

灰色的马一遍又一遍地说这个词。我又重复了一遍，但说得不是很好。棕色的马又说了一个词，一个更难的：Houyhnhnm。我试着说了两三次。最后一次好点儿。

两匹马在说话——关于我的，我心想——然后棕色的马离开了。灰色的马告诉我："我走在前面！"我就跟着他。有时候我走得太慢，他就叫到，"Hhuun, Hhuun"。

"我累了，我走不了更快，"我比画给他看。"我能坐在地上休息会儿吗？"

---

difficult *adj.* 困难的

Then the horse stood *quietly* and I sat down.

We travelled for five kilometres before we arrived at a house. I began to look for people.

"They teach their horses well in this country," I thought. "Now I'll meet the *owner* of this fine horse and he can help me."

But there were no people in the first room of the house — only horses. I followed the horse into the second room, then the third room. I waited for people.

The grey horse made a sound, and a smaller horse and two young horses came. They looked at me.

"This is the horse's house," I thought. "The grey horse is the owner, and these are his wife and children. The servants are horses too. But how can this be true?"

于是这匹马静静地站着，我坐了下来。

我们走了五公里才到达一座房子。我开始寻找人的影子。

"在这个国家，他们把马教导得很好，"我想。"现在我能见到拥有这匹好马的主人了，他能帮助我。"

但在这所房子的第一个房间里没有人——只有马。我跟着马走到第二个房间，然后第三个房间。我期待有人出现。

灰马发出了声音，一匹较小的马和两匹年轻的马来了。他们看着我。

"这是马的房子，"我想。"灰色马是这里的主人，这是他的妻子和孩子。仆人也是马。但是这怎么能是真的呢？"

---

quietly *adv.* 安静地

owner *n.* 主人

The wife looked at me in an *unfriendly* way. She turned to the grey horse and spoke to him. I heard the word Yahoo. He moved his head and said: "Hhuun, Hhuun." So I followed him.

We went to another house, and in it there were three of those ugly, *hairy* animals. They could not leave because there was strong string round them. The other end of the string was in the wall.

The grey horse called a young red-brown horse (a servant), and the servant untied one of the animals. He put that ugly, hairy animal next to me!

The owner and his servant looked carefully at the animal, then at me. Again, I heard the word Yahoo. Then I understood. This ugly

---

灰马的妻子以不友好的方式看着我。她转向灰马并说了些什么。我听见了Yahoo这个词。他摇摇头说："Hhuun，Hhuun。"所以我就跟着他走了。

我们去了另一间房子，那里面有三只丑陋的、多毛的动物。他们不能离开，因为在他们身上捆着牢固的绳子。绳子的另一端拴在了墙上。

灰马叫来一匹年轻的红棕色的马（仆人），这个仆人解开了其中一只动物的绳子。他把那个丑陋的、多毛的动物放在了我旁边！

主人和仆人仔细地看了看动物，又看了看我。我再次听见了Yahoo这个词。然后我就明白了。这个丑陋的动物跟人并没有很大的不同！他有

---

unfriendly *adj.* 不友好的   hairy *adj.* 多毛的

animal was not very different from a man! He had front feet and I had hands. My feet and the Yahoo's feet were the same. The horses could not see that, because I *wore* shoes. Our bodies were the same too. But the horses could not see that because I wore clothes.

The red-brown horse gave me different foods. The Yahoos ate meat, but I could not eat it. It was too hard and dirty. Then the horse gave me horse-food, but it was too *dry* for me.

"I'll have to meet some men," I thought, "or I'll die. And these Yahoos are not men."

前脚，我有手。我的脚和Yahoo（野胡）的脚是一样的。这些马是看不到的，因为我穿着鞋子。我们的身体也是一样的。但是这些马也无法看到，因为我穿着衣服。

红棕色的马给了我不同的食物。"野胡"吃肉，但我吃不了。它太硬太脏了。于是马给了我马吃的草料，但是对我来说又太干了。

"我必须遇到些人，"我想，"否则我会死的。这些'野胡'都不是人类。"

---

wear *v.* 穿   dry *adj.* 干的

I put my hands to my mouth: "I am *thirsty*." The horses gave me milk. Later I made bread from the dry horse-food. Sometimes I caught a bird or a small animal and ate that. With this food and some fruit from the trees, I lived a very good life. I was never ill on that island.

At night, the grey horse — I will call him my owner — talked to his servants about me. They found a place for me near the horse's house, and not too near the Yahoos. I slept there.

我把手指向我的嘴："我渴了。"马给了我牛奶。后来我用干草料做面包吃。有时我抓到一只小鸟或小动物吃。有了这些食物和树上的水果，我生活过得非常好。在那个岛上我从来没有生病过。

晚上，灰马——我会叫他我的主人——跟他的仆人说了关于我的一些事。他们为我找了一个马房近的房子，不是太靠近"野胡"。我就睡在那里。

---

thirsty *adj.* 口渴的

Chapter 2 The Life of the Houyhnhnms

I wanted to learn the language of these horses — the Houyhnhnms. The grey horse, his family and his servants wanted to teach me. Why? Because they wanted the answer to this important question: Can an animal — me — think?

My owner wanted to learn about me, so he gave a lot of time to me.

"You do not walk on your front feet. Why ?" he asked.

"We *call* them hands," I told him, "and we don't walk on them in my country."

第二章 在慧骃国的生活

我想学这些马语——"慧骃语"。灰马，他的家人和他的仆人想教我。为什么呢？因为他们想得到这个重要问题的答案，这个问题就是：一个动物——我——能够思考吗？

我的主人想要了解我，所以他花了很多时间陪我。

"你不用前脚走路。为什么呢？"他问。

"我们把它们叫作手，"我告诉他，"在我的国家我们是不用它们走路的。"

---

call *v.* 把……叫作

"Your nose is too big."

"It is the *right* size for men of my age."

"The Yahoos work for us on the farm, but they do not work well. Nobody can teach them. You are a good Yahoo. You learn and work well."

"But I'm not a Yahoo!" I said *angrily*, when I heard this. "I hate these ugly, dirty animals. You hate them — and I hate them too. Please don't call me a Yahoo!"

My owner wanted to know a lot of things and he asked me a lot of questions: "Where do you come from? Who taught you to think? Nobody can teach the Yahoos to think!"

"你的鼻子太大了。"

"它的大小正适合我这么大年龄的人。"

"'野胡'在农场里为我们工作，但他们不好好工作。没有人可以教他们。你是一个很好的'野胡'。你学习得好也工作得好。"

"但我不是一个'野胡'！"当我听到这个时，我生气地说。"我恨这些丑陋、肮脏的动物。你讨厌他们——我也讨厌他们。请不要叫我'野胡'！"

我的主人想知道很多事，他问了我很多问题："你从哪里来？谁教你思考的呢？没有人能够教会'野胡'思考！"

---

right *adj.* 适当的   angrily *adv.* 生气地

"I came over the sea from another country in a ship. We make ships from wood," I told him. "The other men on the ship brought me here and went away."

"It is not possible," he answered. "No animal can make something from wood and go across the sea in it. Your words are a mistake."

I could not understand these last words. Later I understood. There is no word in the Houyhnhmn's language for untrue. They use language because they want somebody to understand. When the speaker's words are not true, the words are *stupid*. They are "a mistake", because the hearer cannot understand him. So why did the speaker speak?

We talked again and again.

"我坐船从另一个国家越洋而来。我们用木头造船，"我告诉他。"船上其他人把我带到了这里，然后就离开了。"

"这是不可能的，"他回答说。"没有动物能用木头做东西并用它穿越海洋的。你的话是错误的。"

我不懂这最后一句话。后来我明白了。"慧骃"的语言里是没有词表达不真实的。他们使用语言是因为他们想让别人理解。当发言者的话不是真的时，那这话就是愚蠢的。它们是"错误"的，因为听者不能理解。那么为什么发言者这么说呢？

我们谈了一次又一次。

---

stupid *adj.* 愚蠢的

"Who are the rulers in your country?" he asked me.

"You call them Yahoos," I answered.

"Do you have Houyhnhnms there?"

"Yes," I said. "We call them horses. There are many horses in my country. Yahoo servants look after them. They give them food and make their beds. "

"We like horses. They are strong and they run well. We sit on them when we travel. And they run and jump for us."

"How can you *use* them in that way?" asked my owner angrily.

The Houyhnhnms use Yahoos. They work on the farms. They pull

"在你的国家谁是统治者？"他问我。

"你们叫他们'野胡'，"我回答说。

"你们那里有'慧骃'吗？"

"是的，"我说。"我们称之为马。在我的国家有许多的马。'野胡'仆人照顾他们。他们给它们食物，并给它们安排睡觉的地方。"

"我们喜欢马。它们很强大，跑得很快。当我们外出的时候，我们就坐在它们上面。它们为我们跑或跳。"

"你们怎么能用那种方式对待他们？"我的主人生气地问。

"慧骃"使用"野胡"。他们在农场里工作。他们拉东西又搬东西。

---

use *v.* 使用

things and carry things. There are houses for them, but the houses are not too near the horses' houses. When they are not working, they stay outside.

The Yahoos love to be dirty, and the Houyhnhnms cannot understand that. Other animals like to be clean. I was clean. In this way I was different from the Yahoos. The Houyhnhnms saw this and liked me for it.

One day, I talked to my owner about the wars in my country.

"We had a long war with another country—France," I told him. "More than a *million* men died."

"Why do you have wars?" he asked.

"Sometimes the rulers want more cities," I answered. "Then a

他们有房子，但房子不会太靠近马的房子。他们不工作时，就待在外面。

"野胡"喜欢肮脏，"慧骃"不能理解。其他动物喜欢干净。我是干净的。这么说来我是不同于"野胡"的。"慧骃"看见了，并喜欢我这样。

有一天，我跟我的主人讨论我的国家的战争。

"我们与另一个国家——法国进行了长期的战争，"我告诉他。"超过一百万人因此而丧生。"

"你们为什么有战争？"他问。

"有时候，统治者希望拥有更多的城市，"我回答。"那么强大的

---

million *n.* 百万

strong country fights a *weak* country. The *winner* takes the weak country and then the other people are his servants."

"But you Yahoos cannot hurt other people with your teeth," he said. "Our Yahoos hurt other Yahoos in this way. Your words are a mistake."

I told him about the guns and gunpowder in my country. "We can kill a lot of people with one big gun."

He stopped me. "I do not like our Yahoos," he said, "they do not think. They are stupid. They fight for food, for the best places or because they want to fight. You Yahoos can think, but why do you fight? That is worse."

国家就会攻打弱小的国家。胜者就占有了弱国，并且其他人就成为他的仆人。"

"但你们'野胡'不会用牙齿伤害其他人，"他说。"我们的'野胡'以这样的方式伤害别人。你的话是假的。"

我告诉他我的国家里一些关于枪支弹药的情况。"我们可以用一个大枪杀死很多人。"

他打断了我的话。"我不喜欢我们的'野胡'，"他说，"他们不懂得思考。他们很愚蠢。他们为食物、最好的地方而战争，或者是因为他们本身就想战争。你们'野胡'可以思考，那么你们为什么要战争？这更糟

weak *adj.* 虚弱的   winner *n.* 胜利者

"He's calling us Yahoos again!" I thought. "I'll tell him about the good things in my country."

So I talked for a long time about our Parliament, our rulers, our laws and our clever men and women.

There is no word for bad in the Houyhnhnms' language, but they use the word yahoo when a worker is stupid (hhnm yahoo), for a child's mistake (whnaholm yahoo), for strong winds and *heavy* rain. They use it when they cut their feet. They use it when they hate something.

糕。"

"他又叫我们'野胡'了！"我心想。"我会告诉他我的国家里美好的事物。"

所以我就花了很长一段时间谈论我们的议会，我们的统治者，我们的法律和我们聪明的男人和女人。

"慧骃"的语言里目前还没有形言坏的词语，但是当工人很愚蠢（hhnm yahoo）、孩子犯了错误（whnaholm yahoo）、有强风或暴雨时，他们使用"yahoo"。当他们切掉自己的脚时就用这个词。当他们讨厌什么东西时就用这个词。

---

heavy *adj.* （程度）超出一般的

The Houyhnhnms teach their young horses well. The young horses have to be clean, friendly and kind, and they have to work hard. They have to be strong and well. Every four years the young Houyhnhnms from everywhere in the country meet for games and running and jumping. When a horse wins, a friend sings a song for him or her.

Every four years, too, there is a Meeting. Then the *heads* of families talk about the country's important problems.

"慧骃"能很好地教导他们年轻的马。年轻的马必须干净、友好和亲切，他们必须努力工作。他们必须坚强和健康。每四年，年轻的"慧骃"从全国各地赶来参加比赛、参加长跑或是跳跃。当一匹马赢了，一个朋友就会为他或她唱一首歌。

同样，每四年有一个会议。然后族长们会谈论国家的重要问题。

---

head *n.* 领导人

Chapter 3 I Come Home Again

Three years after I arrived in this country, the grey horse came back from a Meeting. His face was very sad.

He said to me: "The other Houyhnhnms are not happy. You are better than a Yahoo because you can learn. They know that. But you cannot live in my family because you are not a Houyhnhnm. They are afraid. One day perhaps the Yahoos will fight us, and you will help them. They say you have to leave my house. I do not like this, but please find some *wood*. Make that ship and travel in it across the sea. We will help you. You have to go!"

第三章 再次回家

我来到这个国家三年后，灰马从一个会议回来了。他显得非常伤心。

他对我说："其他的'慧骃'不开心。你比'野胡'好是因为你能够学习。他们知道。但你不能住在我的家里了，因为你不是一个'慧骃'。他们害怕了。可能有一天，'野胡'会攻打我们，你会帮他们。他们说你必须要离开我的房子。我不喜欢这样，但是去找一些木头吧。把它们做成船并乘它穿过海洋吧。我们会帮助你的。你不得不离开！"

wood *n.* 木头

I was as sad as my owner. I liked the Houyhnhnms. They were very kind and they were good friends. They love everybody in their country, not only their families. They do not marry for love; they marry for strong children. I wanted to stay there with them.

When I thought about my family and friends in England, I tought: "In many ways they're as bad as the Yahoos here. I don't like my face or body now. "

"I don't want to go home. I don't want to be a Yahoo."

I *fell* down at the feet of my owner. For a time I wanted to die. Then I got up and said, "I understand. You and the other Houyhnhnms are right. I'm a stupid Yahoo. I'll leave your country."

我跟我的主人一样伤心。我喜欢"慧骃"。他们都非常友善而且都是好朋友。他们爱他们国家里的每一个人，不仅仅是他们的家人。他们不为爱而结婚，他们为了能有强壮的孩子而结合。我想和他们待在一起。

当我想到我英国的家人和朋友时，我想："在很多方面他们跟这里的'野胡'一样糟糕。我不喜欢我现在的脸或身体。"

"我不想回家。我不想成为一个'野胡'。"

我倒在主人的脚上。有一阵儿，我想去死。后来我站起来说，"我理解。你和其他的'慧骃'是对的。我是一个愚蠢的'野胡'。我会离开你们的国家。"

fall *v.* 倒下

"Thank you," answered my owner. "You can have two months. Then you will have to go. Which servants can help you?"

"The young, red-brown horse likes me," I said. "He and I can build the boat."

In six weeks we made a light boat from wood. We put food and milk and water into it.

On February 15th, 1715, I was ready. Early in the morning, my owner and his family came down to the water and watched. The grey horse cried and put his front foot to my mouth. When I moved out to sea, I heard the red-brown horse. He called in his language: "Be *careful*, good Yahoo!"

I was on the sea for many days. I wanted to go to India, but I

"谢谢你，"我的主人回答说。"你有两个月时间。然后你必须离开。哪一个仆人可以帮你？"

"年轻的、红棕色的马喜欢我，"我说。"他和我可以造一条船。"

在六个星期内我们用木头做了一个小船。我们把食物、牛奶和水放在里面。

1715年2月15日，我准备好了。一大早，我的主人和他的家人来到海边送我。灰马哭了，他把前蹄放在我的嘴边。当我驶入大海，我听到了红棕色马的声音。他用自己的语言说："小心点，好'野胡'！"

我在大海上漂了很多天。我想去印度，但是我找不到那个国家。如果

---

careful *adj.* 小心的

could not find that country. I was nearly dead when I saw a ship.

The Yahoos on the ship were good men. But I felt ill when I looked at them. I wanted to jump into the sea.

"I cannot live with Yahoos!" I cried.

But a man stopped me and tied me to my bed.

They spoke to me in the *Portuguese* language. I know this language well and I could understand them. This was very strange for me.

After two or three days, I began to feel better and I told them about the Yahoos.

"This cannot be true!" they cried.

不是看到一艘船，我差点就死了。

　　船上的'野胡'都是好人。但当我看着他们的时候我很难受。我想跳到海里去。

　　"我不能和'野胡'一起生活！"我大声喊叫着。

　　但一个男人拦住我，把我绑在了床上。

　　他们用葡萄牙语对我说话。我很了解这种语言，我能听懂他们说什么。这对我来说很奇怪。

　　过了两三天，我开始感觉好多了，我告诉了他们关于"野胡"的事情。

　　"这不可能是真的！"他们大声喊着。

Portuguese *adj.* 葡萄牙的

I was angry. After my time in the country of the Houyhnhnms, I could only speak true words. But they listened to my story again. They thought carefully about it and said, "This is *possible*!"

I travelled on this ship to Lisbon. There I found a ship for England.

It was very difficult for me. I had to learn to live with men again. In many ways, they are not different from Yahoos.

"But I don't want to live with Yahoos!" I cried. "I want to live with good, kind Houyhnhnms. I hate dirty Yahoos! And I hate bad Yahoos!"

My people make me angry when they are unkind to horses. I bought two horses. I understand them well and they understand me. I talk to them every day. They are good friends. I can never forget the *wonderful* Houyhnhnms.

　　我很生气。在我从"慧骃"国回来后，我只会说真话。但他们再次听了我的故事。他们仔细地想了一下，说，"这是可能的！"

　　我坐着这条船来到了里斯本。在那里我找到了一艘去英国的船。

　　这对于我来说很难。我需要再次学着跟人一起生活。在许多方面，他们和"野胡"没什么不同。

　　"但是我不想跟'野胡'一起生活！"我大声喊着。"我想和友好又善良的'慧骃'一起生活。我讨厌肮脏的'野胡'！我讨厌邪恶的'野胡'！"

　　当人们对不仁慈时，我会生气。我买了两匹马。我理解它们，它们也能理解我。我每天都跟它们交谈。它们是我的好朋友。我永远不会忘记那些令人赞叹的"慧骃"。

---

possible *adj.* 可能的　　　　　　　　　　　　wonderful *adj.* 令人赞叹的

02

The Phantom of the Opera

Chapter 1 The Dancers

"Quick! Quick! Close the door! It's him!" Annie Sorelli ran into the dressing-room, her face white.

One of the girls ran and closed the door, and then they all turned to Annie Sorelli.

"Who? Where? What's the matter?" they cried.

"It's the *ghost*!" Annie said. "In the *passage*. I saw him. He came through the wall in front of me! And…and I saw his face!"

歌剧院的幽灵

第一章 舞蹈演员们

"快！快！关门！是他！"安妮·索雷丽跑进化妆室，脸色苍白。
一个姑娘跑过去把门关上，然后她们都转向安妮·索雷丽。
"谁？在哪里？发生了什么事？"她们叫道。
"有鬼！"安妮说，"在走廊上，我看到他了。他穿过墙壁来到我的面前。我还……还看到了他的脸！"

---

ghost *n.* 幽灵；鬼   passage *n.* 走廊

Most of the girls were afraid, but one of them, a tall girl with black hair, laughed.

"Pooh!" she said. "Everybody says they see the *Opera* ghost, but there isn't *really* a ghost. You saw a shadow on the wall." But she did not open the door, or look into the passage.

"Lots of people see him," a second girl said. "Joseph Buquet saw him two days ago. Don't you remember?"

Then all the girls began to talk at once.

"Joseph says the ghost is tall and he wears a black evening coat."

绝大多数姑娘都很害怕，但她们中的一个高个子的黑发姑娘却大笑起来。

"呸！"她说，"每个人都说他们看到了这个歌剧院的幽灵，但是这里其实没有鬼。你看见的只是墙上的影子。"但是她没有去把门打开，也没有到走廊上去看个究竟。

"许多人都看到过他，"又一个姑娘说，"约瑟夫·比凯两天前也看到过他，你们难道不记得了？"

随后所有的姑娘们立即开始谈论此事。

"约瑟夫说幽灵是个高个子，穿着黑色晚礼服。"

---

opera n. 歌剧院　　　　　　　　　　　　　　　　really adv. 真正地

"...And no eyes — only black holes!"

Then little Meg Giry spoke for the first time. "Don't talk about him. He doesn't like it. My mother told me."

"Your mother?" the girl with black hair said. "What does your mother know about the ghost?"

"She says that Joseph Buquet is a *fool*. The ghost doesn't like people talking about him, and one day Joseph Buquet is going to be sorry, very sorry."

"But what does your mother know? Tell us, tell us!" all the girls cried.

"……而且没有眼睛——只是黑洞！"

接着娇小的梅格·吉丽第一次开口说话了："不要谈论他。他不喜欢。我妈妈告诉我的。"

"你妈妈？"黑头发姑娘问，"关于幽灵的事儿，你妈妈都知道些什么？"

"她说约瑟夫·比凯是个傻瓜。幽灵不喜欢人们谈论他，总有一天约瑟夫·比凯会后悔的，会非常后悔的。"

"但是你妈妈都知道些什么？告诉我们，告诉我们！"所有的姑娘都叫了起来。

---

fool *n.* 傻瓜

"Oh dear!" said Meg. "But please don't say a word to any one. You know my mother is the *doorkeeper* for some of the *boxes* in the Opera House. Well, Box 5 is the ghost's box! He watches the operas from that box, and sometimes he leaves flowers for my mother!"

"The ghost has a box! And leaves flowers in it!"

"Oh, Meg, your mother's telling you stories! How can the ghost have a box?"

"It's true, it's true, I tell you!" Meg said. "Nobody buys tickets for Box 5, but the ghost always comes to it on opera nights."

"So somebody does come there?"

"Why, no! … The ghost comes, but there is nobody there."

"哦，亲爱的！"梅格说，"但是请不要跟任何人说一个字。你们知道我妈妈是歌剧院一些包厢的看门人。瞧！五号包厢就是这幽灵专用的！他在那个包厢看歌剧，并且有时候会留下一些鲜花给我妈妈！"

"幽灵还有包厢！而且在包厢里留下鲜花！"

"哦，梅格，你妈妈在给你讲故事吧！幽灵怎么会有包厢呢？"

"这是真的，这是真的，我告诉你们！"梅格说，"没有人买五号包厢的票，但是这个幽灵却经常在演晚场歌剧时到包厢里来。"

"那么，确实也有人会去那里吧？"

"为什么，不！……只有幽灵来，但是那里一个人也没有。"

---

doorkeeper *n.* 看门的人   box *n.* 包厢

The dancers looked at Meg. "But how does your mother know?" one of them asked.

"There's no man in a black evening coat, with a yellow face. That's all wrong. My mother never sees the ghost in Box 5, but she hears him!"

"He *talks to* her, but there is nobody there! And he doesn't like people talking about him!"

But that evening the dancers could not stop talking about the Opera ghost. They talked before the opera, all through the opera, and after the opera. But they talked very quietly, and they looked behind them before they spoke.

　　舞蹈演员们看着梅格。"但是你妈妈是怎么知道的？"其中一个问道。

　　"这里根本没有穿黑色晚礼服、黄色面孔的男人。那都是瞎扯。我妈妈从来没有在五号包厢里看到过这个幽灵，但是她听到过！"

　　"他跟她说话，但是里面没有人！而且他不喜欢人们谈论他！"

　　但是那个晚上舞蹈演员们却止不住谈论歌剧院幽灵的话题。她们在歌剧开演前谈论着，在整个演出过程中谈论着，在演出结束后还谈论着。但是她们谈话的声音很小，而且她们在说话前总要先注意一下她们的身后的动静。

---

talk to　与……说话

When the opera finished, the girls went back to their dressing-room. Suddenly, they heard somebody in the passage, and Madame Giry, Meg's mother, ran into the room. She was a fat, *motherly* woman, with a red, happy face. But tonight her face was white.

"Oh girls, " she cried. "Joseph Buquet is dead! You know he walked long way down, on the fourth floor under the stage. The other stage workers found his dead body there an hour ago — with a rope around his neck!"

"It's the ghost!" cried Meg Giry. "The ghost killed him!"

当歌剧演出结束的时候，姑娘们回到了她们的化妆室。突然，她们听到走廊上有人，原来是吉丽夫人，梅格的母亲，跑进了房间。她是一个肥胖的、慈母般的妇人，有一张肤色微红的、快乐的脸。然而今晚她的脸色却是苍白的。

"哦，姑娘们，"她叫道，"约瑟夫·比凯死了！要知道他是从高处掉下来的，掉在舞台底下的第四层。其他的舞台杂工一个小时以前在那里发现了他的尸体——有一根绳子绕在他的脖子上！"

"是幽灵！"梅格·古丽叫道，"是那个幽灵杀死了他！"

---

motherly *adj.* 慈母般的

Chapter 2 The Directors of the Opera House

The Opera House was famous, and the directors of the Opera House were very important men. It was the first week of work for the two new directors, Monsieur Armand Moncharmin and Monsieur Firmin Richard. In the directors' office the next day, the two men talked about Joseph Buquet.

"It was an *accident*," Monsieur Armand said angrily. "Or Buquet killed himself."

"An accident? ...Killed himself?" Monsieur Firmin said. "Which story do you want, my friend? Or do you want the story of the ghost?"

第二章 歌剧院的经理们

歌剧院很有名，而歌剧院的经理们也都是些非常显要的人物。这是两位新经理阿尔芒·蒙沙曼先生和菲尔曼·理查德先生上任的第一个星期。第二天，在经理办公室里，这两位先生谈起了约瑟夫·比凯的事。

"这是个意外事故，"阿尔芒先生气愤地说，"要不然比凯就是自杀的。"

"意外事故？……自杀？"菲尔曼先生说，"你想要听哪种故事，我的朋友？或者说你想听听关于幽灵的故事？"

---

director *n.* 经理　　　　　　　　　　　accident *n.* 事故

"Don't talk to me about ghosts!" Monsieur Armand said. "We have 1,500 people working for us in this Opera House, and everybody is talking about the ghost. They're all *mad*! I don't want to hear about the ghost, OK?"

Monsieur Firmin looked at a letter on the table next to him. "And what are we going to do about this letter, Armand?"

"Do?" cried Monsieur Armand. "Why, do nothing, of course! What can we do?" The two men read the letter again. It wasn't very long.

To the new directors,

Because you are new in the Opera House, I am writing to tell

"不要跟我谈关于幽灵的事！"阿尔芒先生说，"这个歌剧院里有一千五百人在为我们工作，每个人都在谈论关于幽灵的事。他们都疯了！我不想听到关于幽灵的事，行不行？"

菲尔曼先生看着他旁边的桌子上一封给他的信。"那对于这封信我们该做些什么，阿尔芒？"

"做些什么？"阿尔芒先生叫道，"为什么，什么也不做，这是当然的！我们又能做些什么呢？"两位先生又读了一遍这封信。信并不是很长。

致新任经理们：

因为你们是歌剧院的新任经理，所以我写信告诉你们一些重要的事

---

mad *adj.* 疯的

you some important things. Never sell tickets for Box 5; that is my box for every opera night. Madame Giry, the doorkeeper, knows all about it. Also, I need money for my work in the Opera House. It is not expensive, and I am happy to take only 20, 000 francs a month. That is all. But please remember, I can be a good friend, and a bad enemy.

O.G.

"Don't sell tickets for Box 5! 20, 000 francs a month!" Monsieur Armand was very angry again. "That's the best box in the Opera House, and we need the money, Firmin! And who is this O. G., eh? Tell me that!"

情。不要出售五号包厢的票：那是我每次观看晚场歌剧的包厢。吉丽夫人，那位看门人，知道这一切。除此之外，我还需要歌剧院的工钱。我要价并不高，一个月拿两万法郎我就感到满足了。就这些。但是请记住，我会是一个好朋友，也会是一个死对头。

O. G. （注：O. G.即Opera Ghost的缩写。）

"不要出售五号包厢的票！两万法郎一个月！"阿尔芒先生又来气了，"那是歌剧院最好的包厢，而且我们需要钱，菲尔曼！谁是这个O. G.啊？告诉我！"

---

expensive *adj.* 贵的

"Opera Ghost, of course," Monsieur Firmin said. "But you're right, Armand. We can do nothing about this letter. It's a *joke*, a bad joke. Somebody thinks we are fools, because we are new here. There are no ghosts in the Opera House!"

The two men then talked about the opera for that night. It was Faust, and *usually* La Carlotta sang Margarita. La Carlotta was Spanish, and the best singer in Paris. But today, La Carlotta was ill.

"Everybody in Paris is going to be at the opera tonight," said Monsieur Armand, "and our best singer is ill. Suddenly! She writes a

---

"自然是歌剧院的幽灵，"菲尔曼先生说，"但你是对的，阿尔芒。我们绝对不能按照信上说的那么做。这是一个玩笑，一个恶毒的玩笑。一些人认为我们是傻瓜，因为我们是新来的。歌剧院里根本就没有幽灵！"

然后这两位先生就谈论起当晚的歌剧来。当晚的歌剧是《浮士德》，通常由拉·卡洛塔演唱玛格丽塔。拉·卡洛塔是西班牙人，是巴黎最好的歌手。但是今天，拉·卡洛塔却病了。

"今晚巴黎的每个人都会到歌剧院来，"阿尔芒先生说，"而我们最好的歌手却病了。她今天上午才突然写信给我们——她病了，她今晚不能

---

joke *n.* 玩笑   usually *adv.* 通常

letter to us just this morning — she is ill, she cannot sing tonight!"

"Don't get angry again, Armand," Monsieur Firmin said quickly. "We have Christine Daaé, that young singer from Norway. She can sing Margarita tonight. She has a good *voice*."

"But she's so young, and nobody knows her! "

"Nobody wants to listen to a new singer."

"Wait and see. Perhaps Daaé can sing better than La Carlotta. Who knows?"

演唱了！"

"不要再生气了，阿尔芒，"菲尔曼先生急忙说，"我们有克丽斯廷·达埃，那个年轻的挪威歌手。她今晚可以演唱玛格丽塔那个角色。她有一副好嗓子。"

"但是她太年轻了，而且没有人知道她！"

"没有人想听一位新歌手的演唱。"

"等着瞧吧。也许达埃会比拉·卡洛塔唱得更好。谁知道呢？"

---

voice *n.* 噪音；声音

Chapter 3 Christine Daaé

Monsieur Firmin was right. All Paris talked about the new Margarita in Faust, the girl with the *beautiful* voice, the girl with the voice of an angel. People loved her. They laughed and cried and called for more. Daaé was wonderful, the best singer in the world!

Behind the stage Meg Giry looked at Annie Sorelli. "Christine Daaé never sang like that before." she said to Annie. "Why was she so good tonight?"

"Perhaps she's got a new music teacher," Annie said.

第三章 克丽斯廷·达埃

菲尔曼先生说对了。整个巴黎都在谈论歌剧《浮士德》中玛格丽塔的新演唱者，那个有着美妙歌喉的姑娘，那个有着天使一般嗓音的姑娘。人们热爱她。他们笑啊喊啊请求再多唱几曲。达埃的演唱确实不错，她是世界上最好的歌手！

在舞台的后面梅格·吉丽看着安妮·索雷丽。"克丽斯廷·达埃以前从来没有唱得那么好，"她对安妮说，"为什么她今晚唱得这么好呢？"

"或许她有了一位新的音乐老师。"安妮说。

---

beautiful *adj.* 美妙的

The noise in the Opera House went on for a long time. In Box 14, Philippe, the *Comte* de Chagny, turned to his younger brother and smiled.

"Well, Raoul, what did you think of Daaé tonight?"

Raoul, the *Vicomte* de Chagny, was twenty—one years old. He had blue eyes and black hair, and a wonderful smile. The Chagny family was old and rich, and many girls in Paris were in love with the young Vicomte. But Raoul was not interested in them.

He smiled back at his brother. "What can I say? Christine is an angel, that's all. I'm going to her dressing-room to see her tonight."

Philippe laughed. He was twenty years older than Raoul, and was

---

歌剧院里的喧闹声持续了很长一段时间。在十四号包厢里，菲利普，这位沙尼家族的伯爵，微笑着转向他的弟弟。

"嘿，拉乌尔，你觉得今晚达埃表演得怎么样？"

拉乌尔，这位沙尼家族的子爵，二十一岁了。他蓝眼睛黑头发，有着迷人的微笑。沙尼家族古老而富有，巴黎的许多姑娘都爱上了这位年轻的子爵，但是拉乌尔对她们并不感兴趣。

他对他的哥哥报以微笑。"我能说什么呢？克丽斯廷是一位天使，就这样。今晚我要去她的化妆室拜访她。"

菲利普笑了。他比拉乌尔大二十岁，与其说是拉乌尔的兄长，倒不如

Comte *n.* 伯爵   Vicomte *n.* 子爵

more like a father than a brother.

"Ah, I understand," he said. "You are in love! But this is your first night in Paris, your first visit to the opera. How do you know Christine Daaé?"

"You remember four years ago, when I was on *holiday* by the sea, in Brittany?" Raoul said. "Well, I met Christine there. I was in love with her then, and I'm still in love with her today!"

The Comte de Chagny looked at his brother. "Mmm, I see," he said slowly. "Well, Raoul, remember she is only an opera singer. We know nothing about her family."

说是他的父亲。

"啊，我明白了，"他说，"你恋爱了！但是这是你在巴黎的第一个夜晚，你第一次来歌剧院。你是如何认识克丽斯廷·达埃的呢？"

"你还记得4年前，我在布列塔尼海边度假的时候吗？"拉乌尔说，"喔，我在那儿遇见了克丽斯廷。当时我就爱上了她，而且今天我还爱着她！"

这位沙尼家族的伯爵看着他的弟弟。"嗯，我明白了，"他一字一顿地说，"噢，拉乌尔，记住，她只是一个歌剧演员。我们对她的家庭一无所知。"

---

holiday *n.* 假期

But Raoul did not listen. To him, good families were not important, and young men never listen to their older brothers.

There were many people in Christine Daaé's dressing-room that night. But there was a doctor with Christine, and her beautiful face looked white and ill. Raoul went quickly across the room and took her hand.

"Christine! What's the matter? Are you ill?" He went down on the floor by her chair. "Don't you remember me Raoul de Chagny, in Brittany?"

Christine looked at him, and her blue eyes were afraid. She took her hand away. "No, I don't know you. Please *go away*. I'm not well."

但是拉乌尔没听进去。对他来说，好的家庭并不重要，而且年轻人从来都听不进他们兄长的劝告。

那天晚上克丽斯廷·达埃的化妆室里有很多人。但是克丽斯廷的身边还有一位医生，而且她美丽的面容带有病色，显得苍白。拉乌尔快步穿过房间，握住她的手。

"克丽斯廷！怎么了？你病了吗？"他俯下身去靠近她的座椅，"你不记得我了——沙尼家族的拉乌尔，在布列塔尼？"

克丽斯廷看着他，她那双蓝色的眼睛带着惊恐。她把她的手抽走。"不，我不认识你。请走吧。我身体不太好。"

---

go away 离开

Raoul stood up, his face red. Before he could speak, the doctor said quickly, "Yes, yes, please go away. Everybody, please leave the room. *Mademoiselle* Daaé needs to be quiet. She is very tired."

He moved to the door, and soon everybody left the room. Christine Daaé was alone in her dressing-room.

Outside in the passage the young Vicomte was angry and unhappy. How could Christine forget him? How could she say that to him? He waited for some minutes, then, very quietly and carefully, he went back to the door of her dressing-room. But he did not open the door, because just then he heard a man's voice in the room!

拉乌尔站起来，他的脸红了。他还没来得及说话，那位医生就急忙抢着说："对，对，请走吧。各位，请离开房间。达埃小姐需要安静。她太累了。"

他走向门口，不久所有的人都离开了那个房间，只留下克丽斯廷·达埃独自在她的化妆室里。

在门外的走廊上年轻的子爵感到不悦和扫兴。克丽斯廷怎么会忘了他？她怎么会对他说那些话？他等了几分钟，然后，轻轻地，小心翼翼地，他又走回到她的化妆室的门口。但是他没有把门推开，因为就在这个时候，他听到屋里有一个男人的声音！

Mademoiselle *n.* 小姐

"Christine, you must love me!" the voice said.

Then Raoul heard Christine's voice. "How can you talk like that? When I sing only for you…? Tonight, I gave everything to you, everything. And now I'm so tired." Her voice was unhappy and afraid.

"You sang like an angel," the man's voice said.

Raoul walked away. So that was the answer! Christine Daaé had a lover. But why was her voice so unhappy? He waited in the *shadows* near her room. He wanted to see her lover — his *enemy*!

After about ten minutes Christine came out of her room, alone,

"克丽斯廷，你必须爱我！"那个声音说。

接着拉乌尔听到克丽斯廷的声音。"你怎么能那样跟我说话？什么时候我只为你歌唱……？今晚，我把一切都给了你，一切。而现在我太累了。"她的声音显得愁苦而害怕。

"你唱得像一位天使。"那个男人的声音说。

拉乌尔走开了。这样看来那就是答案！克丽斯廷有一个情人。但是为什么她的声音显得如此不开心？他在她房间附近的一处阴影里等着。他要看看她的情人——他的情敌！

过了十分钟左右，克丽斯廷从她的房间里出来了。她独自一人，从走

shadow *n.* 影子

enemy *n.* 敌人

and walked away down the passage. Raoul waited, but no man came out after her. There was nobody in the passage, so Raoul went quickly up to the door of the dressing-room, opened it and went in. He closed the door quietly behind him, then called out:

"Where are you? I know you're here! Come out!"

There was no answer. Raoul looked everywhere — under the chairs, behind all the clothes, in all the dark *corners* of the room. There was nobody there.

廊下去了。拉乌尔等着，但是没有男人跟着她出来。走廊上没有人，于是拉乌尔快步来到化妆室门前，推门而入。他轻轻地把身后的门关上，然后喊道：

"你在哪里？我知道你在这儿！出来！"

没有回答。拉乌尔找遍了所有地方——椅子下面、所有的衣服背后、房间里的每一个阴暗角落。但毫无人影。

---

corner *n.* 角落

Chapter 4 The Phantom is Angry

That was Tuesday night. On Wednesday morning Monsieur Armand and Monsieur Firmin were happy men. Paris liked the new Margarita — everything in life was good. The next opera night was Friday. It was Faust again, but this time with La Carlotta singing Margarita.

By Wednesday afternoon they were not so happy. A second letter arrived for them — from O. G..

Why don't you listen to me? I am getting *angry*. Leave Box 5 free for me. And where are my 20, 000 francs? On Friday Daaé must

---

第四章 幽灵发怒了

那是星期二的晚上。星期三上午阿尔芒先生和菲尔曼先生成了快乐的人。巴黎喜欢玛格丽塔的新演唱者——生活中的一切都是美好的。下一场晚场歌剧是在星期五，还是《浮士德》，但是这一次由拉·卡洛塔演唱玛格丽塔。

星期三下午他们就不那么快乐了。第二封信送到了他们手中——来自 O. G. 的信。

你们为什么不听我的话? 我会发怒的。把五号包厢空着留给我。另外我的两万法郎在哪里? 星期五达埃必须再次演唱玛格丽塔。她是当今巴黎最好的歌唱

---

angry *adj.* 生气的

sing Margarita again. She is now the best singer in Paris. La Carlotta cannot sing — she has a very ugly voice, like a *toad*.

Remember, I am a bad enemy.

"So, Firmin, is this still a joke?" Monsieur Armand shouted. "What are we going to do now, eh? Is O. G. the director here, or are we?"

"Don't shout, Armand," said Monsieur Firmin tiredly. "I don't know the answers. Let's talk to Madame Giry, the doorkeeper of Box 5. Perhaps she can help us."

But Madame Giry was not helpful. Madame Giry was not afraid of ghosts, and she was not afraid of directors of Opera Houses.

家。拉·卡洛塔不能演唱——她的声音非常难听, 活像一只癞蛤蟆。

记住, 我是一个死对头。

"如此看来, 菲尔曼, 这仅仅是一个玩笑吗? "阿尔芒先生喊道, "现在我们该做些什么, 啊? O. G. 是这里的经理, 还是我们? "

"不要喊, 阿尔芒, "菲尔曼先生有气无力地说, "我也不知道如何是好。让我们同吉丽夫人, 那个五号包厢的看门人谈一谈。或许她能帮助我们。"

但是吉丽夫人帮不了什么。吉丽夫人并不怕幽灵, 也不怕歌剧院的经理们。

---

toad *n.* 癞蛤蟆; 蟾蜍

"People say that you're a friend of the Opera ghost, Madame Giry," Monsieur Armand began. "*Tell* us about him. Some people say he has no head."

"And some people say he has no body," said Monsieur Firmin. "What do you say, Madame Giry?"

Madame Giry looked at the two men and laughed. "I say that the directors of the Opera House are fools!"

"What!" Monsieur Armand shouted. He stood up, and his face was red and angry. "Listen to me, woman——"

"Oh, sit down, Armand, and listen," said Monsieur Firmin. "Why do you say that, Madame Giry?"

"人们说你是歌剧院幽灵的朋友，吉丽夫人，"阿尔芒先生打开了话题，"告诉我们有关他的情况。有人说他没有脑袋。"

"也有人说他没有身体，"菲尔曼先生说，"你说呢，吉丽夫人？"

吉丽夫人看着这两个人大笑起来。"我说歌剧院的经理们都是傻瓜！"

"什么！"阿尔芒先生喊道。他站了起来，满脸通红，面显怒色。"听我说，女人——"

"哦，坐下，阿尔芒，听她说，"菲尔曼先生说，"你为什么那样说，吉丽夫人？"

---

tell *v.* 告诉

"Because, Monsieur, the Opera ghost is angry with you. When the ghost wants something, he must have it. He is clever and dangerous, this ghost. The old directors before you, they knew that, oh yes. at first they tried to stop him. Then there were many accidents in the Opera House, many strange accidents. And when did these accidents *happen*? When the ghost was angry! So, the old directors learnt very quickly. The ghost wants Box 5? He can have it every night. The ghost wants money? Let's give the money to him at once. Oh yes, the old directors understood very well."

"But we are the directors, not the Opera ghost!" Monsieur Armand shouted. He turned to Monsieur Firmin. "This woman is

"因为，先生，这歌剧院的幽灵对你们发怒了。当这幽灵想要什么的时候，他就必须得到它。他是聪明而危险的，这个幽灵。你们的那些前任都深谙此道，哦，对了。刚开始他们试图阻止他。但接着在歌剧院里就发生了许多事故，许多意想不到的事故。而那些事故是什么时候发生的呢？就是这幽灵发怒的时候！所以，那些老经理们很快就知道该怎么做了。幽灵想要五号包厢？他可以每个晚上都拥有它。幽灵想要钱？让我们马上把钱给他。哦，对了，那些老经理们领会得很好。"

"但是经理是我们，不是歌剧院的幽灵！"阿尔芒先生喊道。他转向菲尔曼先生。"这个女人疯了。我们为什么要听她的？星期五晚上由拉·卡洛塔

happen *v.* 发生

mad. Why do we listen to her? On Friday night La Carlotta is going to sing Margarita. And you and I, Firmin, are going to watch the opera from Box 5."

"Well, we can *try* that, Armand. But we don't want any accidents."

Madame Giry came nearer to the two men. "Listen to me," she said quietly. "Remember Joseph Buquet? I tell you, the Opera ghost is a good friend, and a bad enemy."

The two men stared at her. "Those words," Monsieur Firmin said slowly," why did you say those words, Madame Giry?"

"Because the ghost says them to me. I never see him, but I often hear him. He has a very nice voice and he doesn't shout at people."

演唱玛格丽塔。而你和我，菲尔曼，就到五号包厢里去观看歌剧。"

"好，我们可以那样试试，阿尔芒。但是我们不希望发生任何事故。"

吉丽夫人走近这两个人。"听我说，"她轻声道："记得约瑟夫·比凯吗？我告诉你们，这歌剧院的幽灵会是一位好朋友，但也会是一个死对头。"

这两个人凝视着她。"那些话，"菲尔曼先生一字一顿地说，"你为什么说那些话，吉丽夫人？"

"因为幽灵跟我说过那些话。我从来没见过他，但是我经常听到他说话。他有一副好嗓子——而且也不对人喊叫。"

---

try *v.* 尝试

Chapter 5 A Letter for Raoul

That Wednesday a letter also arrived for the young Vicomte de Chagny.

He opened the letter, saw the name at the bottom, and smiled for the first time that day.

Dear Raoul ,

Of course I remember you! How could I forget you?

Meet me on Thursday at three o'clock in the Tuileries Gardens. Don't be angry with me, Raoul, please.

Christine Daaé

Raoul put the letter carefully into his *pocket*. Angry? How could

---

第五章 一封致拉乌尔的信

那个星期三也有一封信到了年轻的沙尼家族的子爵手里。

他打开信，看到信末尾的署名，露出了那天的第一个微笑。

亲爱的拉乌尔：

我当然记得你！我怎么会忘了你呢？

星期四下午3点到杜伊勒利花园来见我。请不要生我的气，拉乌尔。

克丽斯廷·达埃

拉乌尔小心翼翼地把这封信放进他的衣服口袋里。生气？他怎么会生

---

pocket *n.* 口袋

he be angry with an angel? On Thursday he was in the Tuileries Gardens by two o'clock.

At ten past three he began to feel unhappy. At half past three he wanted to die, or to kill somebody.

And then... she came. She ran through the gardens to him, and in a second she was in his arms.

"Oh, Christine!" he said, again and again. "Oh, Christine!" They walked through the gardens together and talked for a long time. They remembered their happy weeks in Brittany, four years ago.

"But why did you go away, Christine?" Raoul asked. "Why didn't you *write to me*?"

一位天使的气呢？星期四他两点就到了杜伊勒利花园。

3点过10分的时候他开始感到不快。到3点30分的时候他想死掉，或者杀人。

然后……她来了。她穿过花园奔向他，一下子扑到他怀里。

"哦，克丽斯廷！"他一遍又一遍地说，"哦，克丽斯廷！"他们一同穿过花园并且谈了很长时间。他们回忆起四年前在布列塔尼的快乐时光。

"但是为什么你离开那里了，克丽斯廷？"拉乌尔问，"你为什么不给我写信？"

---

write to sb　给……写信

For a minute or two Christine said nothing. Then she said *slowly*,"We were so young, you and I. I was just a poor singer from Norway, and you…you were the Vicomte de Chagny. I knew I could never be your wife."

"But I love you, Christine——"

"No, shh. Listen to me, Raoul, please. I went home to Norway, and a year later, my father died. I was very unhappy, but I came back to France, to Paris. I worked and worked at my singing, because I wanted to be an opera singer. Not just a good singer, but the best opera singer in Paris."

"And now you are," Raoul said. He smiled. "All Paris is at your feet."

克丽斯廷沉默了一两分钟，然后她才慢慢道来："我和你太年轻，我只是一个从挪威来的贫穷的歌手，而你……你是沙尼家族的子爵。我知道我不可能成为你的妻子。"

"但是我爱你，克丽斯廷——"

"不，嘘，别作声，请听我说，拉乌尔。我回到了挪威，一年后，我父亲逝世了。我非常悲伤，但是我回到了法国，来到了巴黎。我拼命地唱啊唱啊，因为我想成为一名歌剧演唱家。不仅仅是优秀的歌手，而是巴黎最好的歌剧演唱家。"

"现在你是了，"拉乌尔说。他微笑着，"整个巴黎都拜倒在你的脚下。"

---

slowly *adv.* 慢慢地

Christine turned her face away and said nothing.

"Christine," Raoul said quietly. "I want to ask you a question. Who was the man in your dressing-room on Tuesday night? Tell me, please!"

Christine stopped and *stared* at him. Her face went white. "What man?" she *whispered*. "There was no man in my dressing - room on Tuesday night."

Raoul put his hand on her arm. "I heard him," he said. "I listened outside the door and heard a man's voice. Who was he?"

"Don't ask me, Raoul! There was a man's voice, yes, but there was no man in my room! It's true! Oh, Raoul, I'm so afraid. Sometimes I want to die."

克丽斯廷转过脸去，沉默不语。

"克丽斯廷，"拉乌尔轻声说，"我想问你一个问题。星期二晚上在你化妆室的那个男人是谁？请告诉我！"

克丽斯廷停下来凝视着他。她的脸变白了。"什么男人？"她低语道，"星期二晚上没有男人在我的化妆室里。"

拉乌尔把手放在她的手臂上。"我听到他的声音了，"他说："我在门外听，听到了一个男人的声音。他是谁？"

"不要问我，拉乌尔！是有一个男人的声音，是，但是我的房间里没有男人！这是真的！哦，拉乌尔，我害怕极了。有时候我真想去死。"

---

stare *v.* 凝视   whisper *v.* 低语

"Who is he? Tell me, Christine, please. I'm your friend, I can help you. Tell me his name!"

"I cannot tell you his name. It's a *secret*, whispered Christine. "I never see him, I only hear his voice. But he is everywhere! He sees everything, hears everything. That's why I didn't speak to you on Tuesday night. He is my music teacher, Raoul. He's a wonderful singer. "

"I sang so well on Tuesday night *because of* him. I am famous because of him. He is my angel of music! And he says he loves me. How can I leave him?"

"他是谁？请告诉我，克丽斯廷。我是你的朋友，我会帮助你。告诉我他的名字！"

"我不能告诉你他的名字。这是一个秘密，克丽斯廷低声道，"我从来没有见过他，我只是听到他的声音。但是他无处不在！他什么都看得到，什么都听得到。那就是我星期二晚上没有和你说话的原因。他是我的音乐老师，拉乌尔。他是一个极好的歌手。

我星期二晚上之所以唱得那么好就是因为他。我之所以出名就是因为他。他是我的音乐天使！而且他说他爱我。我怎么能离开他呢？"

---

secret *n.* 秘密

because of 因为······

Chapter 6 La Carlotta Sings Margarita

On Friday morning La Carlotta had her breakfast in bed. She drank her coffee and opened her morning letters. One letter had no name on it. It was very short.

You are ill. You cannot sing Margarita tonight. Stay at home and don't go to the Opera House. Or accidents can happen. Do you want to lose your voice—for ever?

La Carlotta was very, very angry. She got out of bed *at once* and did not finish her breakfast.

"This is from Christine Daaé's friends, "she thought. 'They want

第六章 拉·卡洛塔演唱玛格丽塔

星期五早晨拉·卡洛塔在床上用早餐。她一边喝咖啡一边拆阅她的晨信。有一封信没有署名。它非常短。

你病了。今晚你不能演唱玛格丽塔。待在家里不要去歌剧院。否则会有意外。你想失声吗? ——永远?

拉·卡洛塔非常非常气愤。她立即下床,连早餐都没有吃完。

"这是克丽斯廷·达埃的朋友写来的,"她想,"他们希望她今晚再次演

---

lose *v.* 失去   at once 立刻;马上

her to sing again tonight. That *Daaé* girl is going to be sorry for this! I, La Carlotta, I am the best opera singer in Paris. And nothing is going to stop me singing Margarita tonight!"

At six o'clock that evening the dancers were in their dressing-room. They talked and laughed and *put on* their red and black dresses for Faust.

But Meg Giry was very quiet.

"What's the matter, Meg?" Annie Sorelli asked.

"It's the Opera ghost,"Meg said. "My mother says he's angry. She's afraid that something's going to happen tonight."

"Oh, pooh!" the girl with black hair said. "Who's afraid of an old ghost?"

唱。那个叫达埃的姑娘将为此而懊悔！我，拉·卡洛塔，才是巴黎最好的歌剧演唱家。没有什么能够阻止我今晚演唱玛格丽塔！"

当天晚上6点钟舞蹈演员们都来到了她们的化妆室。她们一边笑着说话一边穿上她们红黑颜色的《浮士德》歌剧服。

但是梅格·吉丽却一言不发。

"怎么了，梅格？"安妮·索雷丽问。

"是歌剧院的幽灵，"梅洛说，"我妈妈说他发怒了。她担心今晚会有事情发生。"

"哦，呸！"那个黑发姑娘说，"谁会害怕什么老幽灵？"

---

put on 穿上

An hour later Monsieur Armand and Monsieur Firmin went into Box 5 and sat down. They were not afraid of ghosts. Of course not. There were no ghosts in the Opera House.

Then Monsieur Armand saw some flowers on the floor by the door of the box. "Firmin,"he whispered, "did you put those flowers there?"

Monsieur Firmin looked. "No, I didn't, "he whispered back"Did you?"

"Of course not, you fool! Shh, the music beginning."

La Carlotta did not sing for the first hour. There were no strange voices in Box 5, and the two directors began to feel happier. Then La Carlotta *came out* onto the stage, and Monsieur Firmin looked at

---

一个小时以后阿尔芒先生和菲尔曼先生进了五号包厢坐下。他们从不害怕幽灵。当然不害怕。歌剧院里根本就没有幽灵。

随后阿尔芒先生发现包厢门边的地上放着一些鲜花。"菲尔曼,"他轻声问,"是你把那些鲜花放在那里的?"

菲尔曼先生看了看。"不,我没有,"他反过来轻声问:"是你吗?"

"当然不是,你这个傻瓜!嘘,歌剧开始了。"

拉·卡洛塔在开始的一个小时里不演唱。五号包厢里没有异样的声音,于是两位经理开始感觉心情更加愉快了。接着拉·卡洛塔出现在舞台上,这时菲尔曼

---

come out 出现

Monsieur Armand.

"Did you hear a voice *just then*?" he asked quietly.

"No!" Monsieur Armand said, but he looked behind him twice, then three times, and suddenly felt cold.

La Carlotta sang and sang, and nothing happened. Then she began a beautiful love song.

"My love begins to—Co-ack!"

Everybody stared. What was the matter with Carlotta's voice? What was that strange noise—Coack?

Carlotta stopped and began the song again.

"My love begins to—Co-ack! "

先生看着阿尔芒先生。

"刚才你听到说话声了吗？"他轻声问。

"没有！"阿尔芒先生说，但是他往身后看了两次，随后又看了第三次，接着突然感到一丝凉意。

拉·卡洛塔唱啊唱，并没有发生什么事。接着她开始演唱一首优美的爱情歌曲。

"我的爱始于——科-艾克！"

众人面面相觑。卡洛塔的声音怎么了？那个陌生的杂音——科-艾克是什么？

卡洛塔停下来重新开始演唱。

"我的爱始于——科-艾克！"

just then　刚才

"I cannot forget my—Co-ack!"

It was the noise of a toad! People began to talk and laugh. Monsieur Firmin put his head in his hands. Then he felt Monsieur Armand's hand on his arm. There was a voice in the box with them! A man's voice, laughing!

Poor Carlotta tried again, and again.

"I cannot forget my—Co-ack!"

Then the two directors heard the voice again, behind them, in front of them, everywhere. "Her singing tonight is going to bring down the *chandelier*!"

"我无法忘记我的——科-艾克！"

这是癞蛤蟆的鼓噪！人们开始交头接耳并且哄笑。菲尔曼先生把头埋进双手之中。然后他觉得阿尔芒先生把手放在了自己的手臂上。包厢里有一个声音！一个男人的声音，大笑着！

可怜的卡洛塔试了一次又一次。

"我无法忘记我的——科-艾克！"

接着这两位经理又听到了那个声音，它来自身后，身前，各个方向。"今晚她的演唱将会使枝形吊灯落下来！"

---

chandelier *n.* 枝形吊灯

The two directors looked up at the top of the Opera House. Their faces were white. The famous chandelier, with its thousand lights, broke away from its ropes and *crashed* down on to the people below.

That was a *terrible* night for the Paris Opera House. One woman was killed by the chandelier, and many people were hurt. The Opera House closed for two weeks. And La Carlotta never sang again.

　　两位经理抬头朝歌剧院的屋顶看去。他们的脸色变得惨白。那著名的有着上千盏灯的枝形吊灯，竟然脱离束缚它的绳索坠落在下面的观众席上。

　　对于巴黎歌剧院来说那是一个可怕的夜晚。一名妇女被枝形吊灯砸死，另外许多人被砸伤。歌剧院为此关闭两周。而拉·卡洛塔从此再没有演唱。

---

crash　*v.* 碰撞　　　　　　　　　　　terrible　*adj.* 可怕的

Chapter 7 My Angel of Music

For a week Raoul saw Christine every day. Some days Christine was quiet and unhappy, some days she laughed and sang. She never wanted to talk about Opera House, or her singing, or Raoul's love for her. Raoul was very afraid for her. Who, or what, was this strange teacher, this man's voice, her 'angel of music'?

Then one day there was no Christine. She was not at her home, not at the Opera House, not at their meeting *places*. Raoul looked everywhere

第七章 我的音乐天使

在一个星期的时间里拉乌尔天天都与克丽斯廷约会。有时候克丽斯廷显得沉默而不太高兴，而有时候她又笑又唱。她从不愿提及歌剧院，不愿提及她的演唱，也不愿提及拉乌尔对她的爱。拉乌尔非常为她担心。这个奇怪的老师，这个男人的声音，她的"音乐天使"到底是谁，或者是什么？

后来有一天克丽斯廷不见了。她不在家里，不在歌剧院里，也不在他们约会的地方。拉乌尔到处找并且问遍了所有的人。克丽斯廷·达埃在哪

place *n.* 地方

and asked everybody. Where was Christine Daaé? But nobody knew.

Two days before the Opera House opened again, a letter arrived for Raoul. It was from Christine.

Meet me in an hour at the top of the Opera House, on the tenth floor.

The tenth floor of the Opera House was a dangerous place. There were hundreds of ropes going down to the stage, below it was a long, long way down.

Raoul and Christine sat in a dark corner, and Raoul took Christine's hands. Her face was white and tired.

"Listen, Raoul," she said quiety. "I'm going to tell you everything.

里？但是没有人知道。

在歌剧院重新开业的前两天，一封信送到了拉乌尔手里。它是克丽斯廷写来的。

一个小时以后到歌剧院的顶层第十层来见我。

歌剧院的第十层是一个危险的地方。那里有数百条绳索垂向下面的舞台——长长地下垂着。

拉乌尔和克丽斯廷坐在一个阴暗的角落里，拉乌尔握着克丽斯廷的双手。她的脸色苍白，显得有些疲惫。

---

floor *n.* 楼层

But this is our last meeting. I can never see you again."

"No, Christine!" Raoul cried. " I love you, and we——"

"Shh! Quietly! Perhaps he can hear us. He's everywhere in the Opera House, Raoul!"

"Who? What are you talking about, Christine?"

"My angel of music. I couldn't meet you last Saturday because he came for me, and took me away. I was in my dressing - room in the Opera House and suddenly, he was there in front of me! I saw the voice for the first time! He wore black evening clothes and a *mask* over his face. He took me through many secret doors and passages, down, down under the Opera House. There is a *lake* down there, a

---

"听着，拉乌尔，"她轻声说，"我会把一切都告诉你。但是这是我们的最后一次约会。我再也不能见你了。"

"不，克丽斯廷！"拉乌尔喊道，"我爱你，而且我们——"

"嘘！小声点！也许他能听见。在歌剧院他无处不在，拉乌尔！"

"谁？你在说什么，克丽斯廷？"

"我的音乐天使。上个星期六我没能来见你，因为他来邀我，并且把我带走了。当时我正在歌剧院我的化妆室里，突然地，他就出现在了我的面前！我第一次看到了发出这个声音的人！他穿着黑色晚礼服，脸上戴着面罩。他带着我穿过许多秘密的门和走廊，在歌剧院的底下一直往下、往

---

mask *n.* 面罩；面具

lake *n.* 湖

big lake; the waters are black and cold. He took me across the lake in a boat to his house. He lives there, Raoul, in a house on the lake, under the Opera House!"

Raoul stared at her. Was his beautiful Christine mad? Christine saw his face, and said quickly:

"It's true, Raoul, It's true! And he…, he is the Phantom of the Opera! But he's not a ghost, he's not an angel of music, he's a man! His name is Erik, and he loves me, he wants me to be his wife! No, Raoul, listen, there is more. He told me all this in his house, in a beautiful room. He said that no woman could ever love him, because of his face. He was so unlucky! Then he took off his mask, and I saw

下走。那里的最下面有一个湖，一个挺大的湖；湖水又黑又凉。他用小船带着我划过那个湖去了他的住处。他住在那里，拉乌尔，住在湖上的房子里，在歌剧院的底下！"

拉乌尔凝视着她。他美丽的克丽斯廷疯了吗？克丽斯廷看着他的脸，急切地说：

"这是真的，拉乌尔，这是真的！而且他……他就是那个歌剧院的幽灵！不过他不是鬼，他也不是音乐天使，他是一个实实在在的男人！他的名字叫埃里克，他爱我，他希望我成为他的妻子！不，拉乌尔，听着，还有。在他的房子里，在一个漂亮的房间里，他把这一切都告诉了我。他说

his face."

She began to cry, and Raoul put his arms around her.

"Oh Raoul, he has the most terrible face! It is so ugly! I wanted to *scream* and run away. But where could I run to? He has the face of a dead man, Raoul, but he is not dead! He has no nose, just two black *holes* in his yellow face. And his eyes! Sometimes they are black holes, sometimes they have a terrible red light…"

She put her face in her hands for a second. Then she said, "I stayed in his house for five days. He was very good to me, and I felt sorry for him, Raoul. He wants me to love him, and I told him…I told him…"

没有一个女人曾经爱过他，都是因为他的脸。他是如此的不幸！接着他摘下他的面罩，我看到了他的脸。"

她开始哭起来，拉乌尔一把将她抱住。

"哦！拉乌尔，他有一张最最可怕的脸！它是如此的丑陋！我真想尖叫着跑掉，可是我能往哪儿跑？他有一张死人一样的脸，拉乌尔，但是他并不是死人！他没有鼻子，在他黄色的脸上只有两个黑洞。而他的眼睛！有时候它们是黑洞，有时候它们则发出可怕的红光……"

她把脸埋入双手之中，片刻之后她说："我在他的房子里待了五天。他对我非常好，我觉得对不起他，拉乌尔。他希望我爱他，而我告诉

---

scream *v.* 尖叫

hole *n.* 洞

"No, Christine, no! You're going to be my wife! Come away with me at once, today! You can't *go back* to him."

"But I must," Christine said quietly. "He knows about you, Raoul. He knows about us. He says he's going to kill you. I must go back to him ."

"Never!" said Raoul. "I love you, Christine, and I'm going to kill this Erik!"

"Erik…Erik…Erik…Erik…" The word whispered round the Opera House. Raoul and Christine stared.

"What was that?" Raoul said, afraid. "Was that… his voice?

他……我告诉他……"

"不，克丽斯廷，不！你将成为我的妻子！来，马上和我离开这儿，今天！你不能回到他那儿去。"

"但是我必须，"克丽斯廷轻声道，"他知道你，拉乌尔。他知道我们的事。他说他要杀了你。我必须回到他那儿去。"

"决不！"拉乌尔说，"我爱你，克丽斯廷，而且我要杀了这个埃里克！"

"埃里克……埃里克……埃里克……埃里克……"这声音在歌剧院里低声回荡着。拉乌尔和克丽斯廷面面相觑。

---

go back 回去

Where did it come from?"

"I'm afraid, Raoul, "Christine whispered. "I'm singing Margarita again on Saturday. What's going to happen?"

"This," Raoul said. "After the opera on Saturday night, you and I are going away together. Come on, let's go down now. I don't like it up here."

They went carefully *along* a dark passage to some stairs, then suddenly stopped. There was a man in front of them, a tall man in a long dark coat and a black hat. He turned and looked at them.

"No, not these stairs," he said. "Go to the stairs in the front. And

---

　　"那是什么？"拉乌尔害怕地说，"那是……他的声音吗？它是从哪儿传出来的？"

　　"我害怕，拉乌尔，"克丽斯廷轻声说，"星期六我将再次演唱玛格丽塔。到时候会发生什么事呢？"

　　"这样，"拉乌尔说，"演完星期六晚上的那场歌剧以后，你和我一起离开这儿。来，我们现在下去吧。我不喜欢待在这儿。"

　　他们小心翼翼地沿着黑暗的走廊朝楼梯走去，接着突然停住了。一个男人站在他们前面，一个高个子男人，穿着深色长外衣，戴着一顶黑色帽子。他转过身来看着他们。

---

along *prep.* 沿着；顺着

go quickly!"

Christine turned and ran. Raoul ran after her.

"Who was that man?" he asked.

"It's the *Persian*," Christine answered.

"But who is he? What's his name? Why did he tell us to go to the front stairs?"

"Nobody knows his name. He's just the Persian. He's always in the Opera House. I think he knows about Erik, but he never talks about him. Perhaps he saw Erik on those stairs, and wanted to help

---

"不，别走这楼梯，"他说，"去前面那楼梯，快走！"

克丽斯廷转身就跑。拉乌尔跟着她跑。

"那个人是谁？"他问。

"是个波斯人。"克丽斯廷回答。

"但是他是谁？他叫什么名字？为什么他告诉我们要走前面的楼梯？"

"没有人知道他的名字。他就是波斯人。他经常在歌剧院里。我想他了解埃里克，但是他从不提及他。或许他看到埃里克在那楼梯上，想帮助我们。"

Persian *n.* 波斯人

us."

Hand in hand, they ran quickly down the stairs, through passages, then more stairs and more passages. At one of the little back doors to the Opera House, they stopped.

"On Saturday night, then. After the opera," Raoul said. " I'm going to take you away, and marry you."

Christine looked up into his face. "Yes, Raoul."

Then they *kissed*, there by the door of the Opera House. That was their first kiss.

他们手拉着手飞快地跑下楼梯，穿过走廊，下面还有更多的楼梯和走廊。在快到歌剧院小后门口的一道门那儿，他们停住了。

"星期六晚上，到那时，演完歌剧以后，"拉乌尔说，"我要带你离开这儿，并且和你结婚。"

克丽斯廷抬头深情地看着他的脸。"好吧，拉乌尔。"

随后他们接吻了，在歌剧院的那道门边。那是他们的初吻。

---

hand in hand　手拉手

kiss　*v.* 接吻

Chapter 8 Where is Christine Daaé?

On Saturday morning Comte Philippe looked across the breakfast table at his brother.

"Don't do it, Raoul, please. All talk about ghosts and phantoms. I think the girl is mad."

"She's not mad, and I'm going to marry her," Raoul said.

"She's only a *little* opera singer," Philippe said unhappily. "And she's very young. Are you still going to love her in ten, or twenty, years time?"

Raoul drank his coffee and did not answer.

第八章 克丽斯廷·达埃哪去了？

星期六早上菲利普伯爵走到早餐桌那头他弟弟的面前。

"请不要做这样的事，拉乌尔。这里所有人都在谈论鬼啊幽灵啊。我想那个姑娘疯了。"

"她没有疯，而且我要和她结婚。"拉乌尔说。

"她只是一个毫不起眼的歌剧演员，"菲利普不高兴地说，"而且她太年轻。十年二十年以后你还会爱她吗？"

拉乌尔喝着咖啡没有回答。

---

little *adj.* 微不足道的

There were two *unhappy* faces in the Opera House, too. The directors now understood about O. G. .They didn't want any more accidents.

"Box 5 is free tonight for O. G.. Daaé is singing Margarita. And here is 20, 000 francs. Madame Giry can leave the money in Box 5 for him. Is that everything?" Monsieur Armand asked Monsieur Firmin.

"It's a lot of money," Monsieur Firmin said unhappily. He thought for a minute. "What about some flowers in Box 5? Madame Giry says that O. G. likes flowers."

"O. G. can bring his own flowers!" shouted Monsieur Armand.

The evening began well. The chandelier was now back in place with

---

在歌剧院里也有两张很不高兴的面孔。经理们现在终于知道了O. G.的厉害。他们不想再出现任何事故。

"五号包厢今晚空着留给O. G. 。由达埃来演唱玛格丽塔。另外，这里是两万法郎。吉丽夫人可以把这些钱留在五号包厢里给他。那些就是所有的事吧？"阿尔芒先生问菲尔曼先生。

"这可是很多钱啊，"菲尔曼先生不高兴地说。他想了一会儿，"在五号包厢里放些鲜花怎么样？吉丽夫人说那个O. G. 喜欢鲜花。"

"O. G. 可以带上他自己的鲜花！"阿尔芒先生喊道。

这个夜晚到来时，一切还是令人满意的。那枝形吊灯换了新的绳索又

---

unhappy *adj.* 不高兴的

new ropes. All Paris was in the Opera House. Everybody wanted to hear Christine Daaé's voice again. People also knew about the love story between Christine Daaé and the Vicomte de Chagny. There are no love secrets in Paris! People watched the Comte and the Vicomte in Box 14 with interest. Usually young men from families like de Chagny do not marry opera singers.

When Christine came onto the stage, her face was white and she looked afraid. But she sang like an angel. Ah, what a voice! All Paris *was in love with* Christine Daaé.

She began to sing the famous love song. Suddenly, every light in

回到了它原来的位置。巴黎所有的人都到了歌剧院。每个人都想再次欣赏克丽斯廷·达埃的演唱。人们也都知道了克丽斯廷·达埃和沙尼家族的子爵之间的爱情故事。在巴黎没有什么爱情秘密！人们饶有兴趣地朝十四号包厢里的伯爵和子爵张望着。出身于像沙尼那样家族的年轻人一般是不会与歌剧演员结婚的。

当克丽斯廷出现在舞台上的时候，她的脸色苍白而且看上去有些害怕。但是她唱得像一位天使。啊，多么美妙的声音！整个巴黎都爱上了克丽斯廷·达埃。

她开始演唱那首著名的爱情歌曲。突然，歌剧院里所有的灯都熄灭

be in love with 爱；喜欢

the Opera House went out. For a second nobody moved or spoke. Then a woman screamed, and all the lights came on again.

But Christine Daaé was no longer on the stage! She was not behind the stage, she was not under the stage. Nobody could find her.

The Opera House went mad. Everybody ran *here and there*, shouted and called. In the directors office, people ran in and out. The police came, and asked questions. But nobody could answer the questions. Monsieur Armand got angry and shouted, and Monsieur Firmin told him to be quiet. Then Madame Giry arrived at the office with her daughter Meg.

了。这片刻之间没有人走动，也没有人说话。随后一个女人尖叫起来，与此同时所有的灯又都亮了。

但是克丽斯廷却不在舞台上了！她不在舞台的后面，也不在舞台底下。没有人能找到她。

歌剧院里乱得一团糟。每个人都跑来跑去，又喊又叫。在经理办公室，人们跑进跑出。警察来了，问了一些问题。但是没有人能够回答这些问题。阿尔芒先生发着脾气，大喊着，菲尔曼先生要他冷静一些。接着，吉丽夫人领着她的女儿梅格走进了办公室。

---

here and there 各处；到处

"Go away, woman!" Monsieur Armand shouted.

"Monsieur, there three people are missing now!" Madame Giry said. "Meg, tell the directors your story."

This was Meg's story.

"When the lights *went out*, we were just behind the stage. We heard a scream — I think it was Christine Daaé's voice. Then the lights came back on, but Christine wasn't there! We were very afraid, and we began to run back to our dressing - room. There were people running everywhere! Then we saw the Vicomte de Chagny. His

---

"出去，你这个女人！"阿尔曼先生喊道。

"先生，现在有三个人失踪了！"吉丽夫人说，"梅格，把你看到的事告诉经理们。"

这是梅格的故事。

"当灯熄灭的时候，我们正在舞台的后面。我们听到一声尖叫——我觉得是克丽斯廷·达埃的声音。随后灯又亮了，但是克丽斯廷不见了！我们非常害怕，都往自己的化妆室跑。人们到处乱跑！接着我们看见了沙尼家族的子爵。他满脸通红显得非常愤怒。"克丽斯廷你在哪里？克丽斯廷你在哪里？"他喊着。突然那个波斯人从他后面走上来抓住

---

go out 熄灭

face was red and he was very angry. "Where's Christine? Where's Christine? "he shouted. *Suddenly* the Persian came up behind him and took his arm. He said something to the Vicomte and they went into Christine Daaé's dressing-room…"

"Yes? And then?" Monsieur Firmin said quickly. "What happened next?"

"Nobody knows!" Meg's face was white. "We looked into Christine Daaé's dressing-room, but…but there was nobody there!"

了他的手臂。他对子爵说了些什么，然后他们就进了克丽斯廷·达埃的化妆室……"

"是吗？那么后来呢？"菲尔曼先生着急地问，"接下来发生了什么事？"

"没有人知道！"梅格脸色苍白，"我们朝克丽斯廷·达埃的化妆室里面看了看，但是……但是那里并没有人！"

---

suddenly *adv.* 突然

Chapter 9 The House on the Lake

When the lights came on, Raoul ran. He ran down stairs and along passages, through the Opera House to the back of the *stage*. In the passage outside Christine's dressing - room, a hand took his arm.

"What's the matter, my young friend? Where are you running to so quickly?"

Raoul turned and saw the long face of the Persian under his black hat.

"Christine!" Raoul said quickly. "Erik's got her. Where is she? Help me! How do I get to his house on the lake?"

第九章 湖面上的房子

当灯亮起的时候，拉乌尔跑了。他跑下楼梯，沿着走廊，穿过歌剧院来到舞台的背后。在克丽斯廷化妆室门外的走廊上，一只手抓住了他的手臂。

"怎么了，我的年轻的朋友？你跑得这么快要去哪儿？"

拉乌尔转过身来看到了那张黑色帽子下波斯人的长脸。

"克丽斯廷！"拉乌尔急切地说，"埃里克把她掳走了。她在哪里？帮帮我！我怎么到他湖上的房子那儿？"

stage *n.* 舞台

"Come with me," said the Persian. They went quickly into Christine's dressing - room. The Persian closed the door and went to the big *mirror* on the wall.

"There's only one door into this room," Raoul began to say.

"Wait," the Persian said. He put his hands on the big mirror, first here, then there. For a minute nothing happened. Then the mirror began to move and turn, and a big dark hole appeared in it. Raoul stared.

"Quick! Come with me, but be careful," the Persian said. "I know Erik. I understand his secrets. Put your right hand up near your head, like this, and keep it there all the time. "But why?" Raoul asked.

"跟我来。"波斯人说。他们飞快地进了克丽斯廷的化妆室。波斯人把门关上,朝墙上的那面大镜子走去。

"进这个房间只有一扇门啊。"拉乌尔忍不住说。

"等一会儿,"波斯人说。他把手放在大镜子上,从一边到另一边。过了一会儿并没有什么动静。接着镜子开始转动起来,里面出现了一个大的黑洞。拉乌尔目瞪口呆。

"快!跟我来,不过小心点,"波斯人说,"我了解埃里克。我知道他的秘密。把你的右手举起来靠近你的头,像这样,并且要一直保持那样。""这是为什么?"拉乌尔问。

---

mirror *n.* 镜子

"Remember Joseph Buquet, and the *rope* around his neck? Erik is a clever man with ropes in the dark."

They went down, down, down, under the Opera House. They went through secret doors in the floors, then along passages and down dark stairs. The Persian listened carefully all the time for strange noises.

"When do we get to the lake?" Raoul whispered.

"We're not going by the lake. Erik watches it all the time. We go round the lake and get into Erik's house from the back. I know some secret doors."

Soon they were there. In the dark, the Persian felt the wall carefully with his hands. "Ah, here it is," he whispered. The wall

---

"还记得约瑟夫·比凯和绕在他脖子上的绳子吗？埃里克是个聪明人，善于在黑暗中使用绳子。"

他们往歌剧院的底下走，往下，一直往下。他们通过一层层密门，接着沿着走廊走下黑暗的楼梯。波斯人一直仔细听着有无异样的声音。

"我们什么时候才能到湖边？"拉乌尔轻声问。

"我们不从湖上走。埃里克一直在那儿看着。我们绕过湖从背后进入埃里克的房子。我知道一些密门。"

不久他们到了那里。黑暗中，波斯人用手仔细地在墙上摸索。"啊，在这里。"他低声道。墙在他手下动起来并且出现了一道小门。他们脚步

---

rope *n.* 绳子

moved under his hands and a small door opened. Very quietly, they went through, and then the door closed behind them. They could not get out.

Inside the room it was very dark. They waited and listened. The Persian put his hands on the wall.

"Oh no!" he whispered. "It was the wrong door! This is Erik's *torture* room — the room of mirrors! We are dead men, Vicomte de Chagny, dead men!"

At first Raoul did not understand. But soon he learnt. The lights came on, and they heard a man's laugh. Erik knew they were there.

The room was all mirrors—walls, floor, *ceiling*. There were pictures in the mirrors of trees and flowers and rivers. The pictures moved and danced in front of their eyes.

很轻地走了进去，然后门在他们的身后关上了。他们不能出去了。

房间里很黑。他们等待着、倾听着。波斯人把手放到了墙上。

"哦，不！"他低声道，"我们走错了一道门！这是埃里克的拷问室——那个都是镜子的房间！我们成了死人了，沙尼家族的子爵，死人！"

一开始拉乌尔还没有明白是怎么回事，但是不久他就意识到了。灯亮了，而且他们听到了一个男人的笑声。埃里克知道他们在那儿。

这个房间里全是镜子——墙，地板，天花板。镜子里有树、鲜花、河流的图画。这些图画在他们的眼前跳动着。

---

torture *n.* 拷问

ceiling *n.* 天花板

The room was hot. It got hotter and hotter and hotter. Raoul was thirsty, hot and thirsty, and the rivers in the pictures danced and laughed at him. He closed his eyes, but the rivers still danced. Water, he *needed* water, but the mirrors laughed at him. Soon he could not move or speak, or open his eyes. He was not thirsty now, just tired, so tired. "Oh Christine, I'm sorry," he thought. "I wanted to help you, but now I'm dying…"

Through a mirror in the wall Christine watched her *lover* in the torture room. Behind her stood Erik , with his hands on her arms.

"He's dying, Christine, dying. Watch him carefully. No, don't close your eyes. Watch him!"

房间里热烘烘的。而且变得越来越热。拉乌尔觉得渴，又热又渴，而图画上的河流跳动着仿佛在嘲笑他。他闭上眼睛，但是河流依旧在晃动着。水，他需要水，但是镜子在嘲笑他。不久他就不能动不能说话，也不能睁眼了。他现在不觉得渴了，只觉得累，累极了。"哦！克丽斯廷，对不起，"他想，"我想帮助你，而现在我快要死了……"

透过墙里的镜子克丽斯廷看着她在拷问室里的情人。她的身后站着埃里克，他的双手放在她的手臂上。

"他快要死了，克丽斯廷，快要死了。仔细地看着他。不，不许闭上眼睛，看着他！"

---

need *v.* 需要　　　　　　　　　　　　　lover *n.* 情人

Christine could not speak. She wanted to scream, but no words came. Then she found her voice again.

"How can you do this, Erik! Why don't you kill me?"

"Because I love you, Christine. *Marry* me, be my wife, and love me. Then Raoul and the Persian can live."

Slowly, Christine turned. She looked into Erok's terrible, ugly face, and spoke again, very quietly.

"Yes, Erik. From this minute I am your wife." She put her arms around Erik's neck, and kissed him—kissed him slowly and lovingly

---

克丽斯廷说不出话来。她想尖叫，但发不出声音。接着她发现自己又能说话了。

"你怎么能这样做，埃里克！你为什么不杀了我？"

"因为我爱你，克丽斯廷。和我结婚吧，做我的妻子，并且爱我。这样拉乌尔和波斯人就能活下来。"

慢慢地，克丽斯廷转过身来。她看着埃里克那可怕、丑陋的脸，又一次开口说话了，非常温和地说。

"好的，埃里克。从这一刻起我就是你的妻子了。"她张开双臂搂住埃里克的脖子，并且吻了他——慢慢地充满爱意地吻了他那丑陋的嘴。随

---

marry *v.* （和某人）结婚；嫁

on his ugly mouth. Then she took her arms away and said slowly, "*Poor*, unhappy Erik."

Erik stared at her. "You kissed me!" He whispered. "I didn't ask you, but you kissed me freely! Oh Christine, my angel! That was my first kiss from a woman. Even my mother never kissed me! She gave me my first mask when I was two years old. She turned her face away from me every time I came near her."

Erik put his ugly face in his hands and cried. Then he went down on the floor at Christine's feet. "You are *free*, Christine, free! Go away and marry your Raoul, and be happy. But remember Erik, sometimes. Go now, quickly! Take Raoul and the Persian, and go!"

后她放下手臂缓缓地说："可怜的不幸的埃里克。"

埃里克凝视着她。"你吻了我！"他轻声道，"我没有要求你，但是你吻了我——自愿地！哦！克丽斯廷，我的天使！这是我从女人那儿得到的第一个吻。即便我的母亲也从来没有吻过我！当我两岁的时候，她给了我第一个面罩。每次我走近她，她都把脸从我那儿转开。"

埃里克把他那丑陋的脸埋进双手哭了起来。随后他伏到克丽斯廷的脚下。"你自由了，克丽斯廷，自由了！去和你的拉乌尔结婚吧，祝你们快乐。不过有的时候不要忘记埃里克。现在就走吧，快！带上拉乌尔和波斯人，走吧！"

poor *adj.* 可怜的　　　　　　　　　free *adj.* 自由的

Chapter 10 Madame Giry Visits the Persian

For weeks, all Paris talked about that night at the opera. Everybody asked questions, but nobody knew the answers. Where was Christine Daaé? Where was the Vicomte de Chagny? Were they *alive*, or dead?

And the Phantom of the Opera...?

Some weeks after that famous night Madame Giry went out one afternoon to a small house near the Rivoli Gardens. She went in and up the stairs to some rooms at the top of the house. The Persian opened the door.

第十章 吉丽夫人拜访波斯人

几个星期以来，整个巴黎都在谈论歌剧院的那个夜晚。每个人都问这问那，但是没有人知道问题的答案。克丽斯廷·达埃哪儿去了？沙尼家族的子爵哪儿去了？他们是活着，还是死了？

还有那歌剧院的幽灵……？

在那个出名的夜晚过去几个星期以后的一天下午，吉丽夫人出门去了里沃利花园附近的一座小房子。她进门上了楼梯来到房子顶层的几个房间前，波斯人打开了房门。

alive *adj.* 活着的

Madame Giry looked at him. "My friend, you know the answers. Please tell me. Are they alive or dead?"

"*Come in*," the Persian said quietly.

They sat down on some chairs by the window, and looked out across the Rivoli Gardens.

"Yes," the Persian said slowly, "The Phantom is dead now. He did not want to live any longer. I saw his body three days ago, and because of that, I can talk to you about him. He cannot kill me now."

"So the Phantom was really a man?" Madame Giry asked.

"Yes, his name was Erik. That was not his real name, of course.

吉丽夫人看着他。"我的朋友，你知道答案。请告诉我，他们是活着还是死了？"

"进来。"波斯人轻声说。

他们在靠近窗口的椅子上坐下，看着窗外的里沃利花园。

"是的，"波斯人缓缓地说，"那个幽灵现在已经死了。他不想再活下去了。我三天前见到了他的尸体，正因如此，我才可以告诉你他的事。他现在不能杀我了。"

"那么那个幽灵真的是一个男人吗？"吉丽夫人问。

"对，他的名字叫埃里克。当然，那不是他的真名。他出生在法国，

---

come in 进来

He was born in France, but I knew him in Persia. He was a famous *builder* and I worked with him there. For a time I was his friend, but not for long. When he came to Paris, I came after him—I wanted to watch him. "

"He was a very clever, very dangerous man. He could be in two, or three places at the same time. He could be in one place, and his voice could come from another place. He could do many clever things with ropes, mirrors and secret doors. You see, he helped to build the Opera House. He built secret passages *underground*, and his secret house on the lake. He could not live in the outside world,

不过我是在波斯认识他的。他是一位著名的建筑师，我在那儿跟他工作。我一度是他的朋友，但是并不长久。当他来巴黎时，我跟随他来了——我想监视他。"

"他是一个非常聪明、非常危险的人物。他能够同时在两个或三个地方出现。他能够做到身在一个地方，而他的声音来自另一个地方。他能利用绳子、镜子和密门做许多巧妙的事情。你看，他帮助建造了歌剧院。他建造了地下的秘密通道和湖上的秘密居所。他不能生活在外面的世界，因为他的可怕、丑陋的脸。不幸的埃里克！我们为他感到难过，吉丽夫人。他是如此聪明……又如此丑陋。人们看到他的脸就尖叫。所以他过着这种

builder *n.* 建筑师　　　　　underground *adv.* 在地下

because of his terrible, ugly face. Unhappy Erik! We feel sorry for him, Madame Giry. He was so clever…and so ugly. People screamed when they saw his face. So he lived this strange life half - man, half -phantom. But he was a man, in the end. He wanted a woman's love…"

He stopped, and Madame Giry asked quietly, "And Christine Daaé and Vicomte Raoul? What happened to them?"

The Persian smiled. "Ah yes! What happened to young Raoul and the beautiful Christine…? Who knows?"

Nobody in Paris ever saw Raoul and Christine again.

Perhaps they took a train to the north, and lived a quiet, happy life together there. Perhaps Christine's wonderful voice is still singing, *somewhere* in the cold and beautiful mountains of Norway. Who knows?

怪异的生活——半人半鬼。但是他终究是个男人。他需要女人的爱……"

他话一停，吉丽夫人就轻声问："那克丽斯廷·达埃和拉乌尔子爵呢？他们怎么样了？"

波斯人微笑着。"啊，对了！年轻的拉乌尔和美丽的克丽斯廷怎么样了……？谁知道呢？"

巴黎没有人再见过拉乌尔和克丽斯廷。

也许他们坐上了北去的火车，在那里一起过着平静、快乐的生活。也许克丽斯廷那美妙的歌喉依然在歌唱，在挪威寒冷而美丽的山里的某个地方。谁知道呢？

---

somehere *pron.* 某处